Daddy's Demands

A True Story

Cheryl Jolly

iUniverse, Inc.
New York   Bloomington

Daddy's Demands
A True Story

Copyright © 2010 Cheryl Jolly

iUniverse books may be ordered through booksellers or by contacting:

iUniverse
1663 Liberty Drive
Bloomington, IN 47403
www.iuniverse.com
1-800-Authors (1-800-288-4677)

ISBN: 978-1-4502-1885-6 (pbk)
ISBN: 978-1-4502-1886-3 (ebk)

Printed in the United States of America

iUniverse rev. date: 6/7/2010

This is a true story.

Please, let us get together and save ourselves, and our children, from physical, mental, and sexual abuse. All we need is love, peace, and understanding

A percentage of the proceeds of this book will be sent to abuse centers and shelters worldwide to help desperate people in need. So that they get the help they need to live a happier life.

This book will hopefully help all our children and adults who feel like they cannot go on anymore. All we need to do is get together and help anyone who we know is in this situation.

If we can learn how to heal our children and ourselves from this torture and pain, then and only then, can we break free to live a better and happier life.

Before I continue this book, I must tell you that I cannot, and will not, reveal the names of any of the people involved. I will not reveal their names because I feel that they themselves were pressured into doing the things they did by my father. I am not saying that these people didn't have a mind of their own but my father had a way about him that not many people could walk away from. I truly believe that most of these people have really learned that what they did was the wrong thing to do to anyone, especially to these poor innocent children. I just pray that they have never harm another child since. Most of the names revealed in this book are fictional.

Introduction

This is a true story about a five year old girl. This girl was molested and mentally abused by her father. The abuse began and continued on until she was fifteen years old. I was this little girl. I am now forty-four years old. I have many experiences in the past that I wish to share with you. My main reason for writing this book is to help anyone, most especially young teenagers, learn how to deal with any type of abuse.

I hope and pray this will help you in some way to talk about and get through this horrible experience. You must understand, no matter what anyone might say, this is in no way your fault. People that tell you otherwise are either in denial or are worried about themselves, worried about getting caught and going to jail; which is where they belong in the first place if this is how they are treating you. Do not ever believe anything different. You and only you must learn how to heal yourself and move forward before you can truly live in peace. Always remember that NO means NO.

Then you can finally be able to forgive.

Dedication

First, I wish to dedicate this book to my one and only daughter, Danielle. If not for her, I believe that I would never have had the strength to write this book. She is only seventeen years old. I have talked to her about many of my experiences to teach her that not all people are trustworthy. For just talking to her about some things has made her understand a lot about how people should be treated. For this, I believe that, in some way, I have helped her from being harmed. I love you with every part of my being.

I also wish to thank my mother who always stood by me and now I see the love she gives me is real. She was also very afraid of my father, as you will read as my story is being told. I never knew that she truly loved me like this but now I do. Thanks for everything, Mom. I also have to thank my two older brothers for if they were not there to protect me on many occasions I might not be here today.

Thanks to my family who helped me in the past and I appreciate all that everyone has done for me.

Thanks to my soul mate, Steve, who I have been with for over fifteen years now. This is the man that wrote the song to my book. I truly love this man with all my heart and soul. He has stayed by my side before and after my accident which left me in a great deal of pain along with the many health problems I have been having ever since.

Thanks for creating this beautiful song for me as it gives me a feeling of helping other people get through any similar experiences they might have gone through. My love to you all and I cannot thank you enough for all of your help as you have saved my life.

Special thanks go to my other four best friends whom I mentioned in this book even if I haven't totally revealed their identities. I grew up with two of them since I was eleven or twelve and the other two were those I have known for the last fifteen years. We have all helped each other in one way or another. Thank you for everyone's help as you have all brought me closer to the Light.

Thank you and I love you always.

Cheryl.

Finally, yet importantly, I do have to thank my father, believe it or not. For if it wasn't for him I might never have had the honor of being able to leave my body and see what I can today. Not only have I learned a lot about life and who I really am, but also have understood the true meaning of my life. That is, to always protect my daughter to the best of my ability, to never live a lie and always be true to myself. I now know that I will always help people in need if I can. I spent my life hating my father but I now finally understand that he was truly sick.

Thank you, Dad, for showing me the true meaning of life.

I AM A SURVIVOR!

Love Cheryl.

The lyrics to
DADDY'S DEMANDS.

She had a life,
A life before I met her,
She had dreams,
Though shattered,
Shattered by her fight.

She remembers,
Like it was yesterday,
All the things he told her,
And how they never went away.

Daddy's Demands are silent,
They echo in the night,
They washed away her innocents,
As she holds it all inside.

Her Daddy's cries are desperate,
And she doesn't know why,
All she wants is to be loved,
But it shouldn't hurt a little child at night.

Thirty years of freedom,
And she still hears his Demands,
All she wanted was a simple life,
Hear in walls from his commands.

But Daddy's Demands are silent,
They echo in the night,
They washed away her innocents,

As she holds it all inside.

Her Daddy's cries are desperate,
And she doesn't know why,
All she wants is to be loved,

But it shouldn't hurt a little child at night.

Thank you so much Steve

Love you always
Cheryl

1
The Child Within

The year was 1968. I was five years old, living with my parents and my two brothers in an apartment complex in a suburban community. My father was the nicest and kindest person you could have ever wanted to meet. At that time, he was someone who had sense of humor and was always there for his little girl.

I loved and trusted him. He was a short, dark haired husky man. I got my looks from him. He worked very hard through the week to provide for us while my mother had just started her first job after I, being the youngest in the family, started school. That year my father taught me that you cannot trust anyone. Not even your own father who most children would automatically assume would protect them at any cost.

My father was an alcoholic for as long as I could remember. Mind you, he only drank on weekends so I believed that this meant that he was a weekend alcoholic. He never drank during the week as he was a plant manager of a very large company.

He always provided for us all very well despite his drinking problem. During the week, when he was sober, no one could ever guess what a monster he was. When the weekend came along, he was a totally different person that not many people knew about. We also were never allowed to talk about the way we really lived.

The first incident of abuse that I remembered was when I was five years old. I still remember it like it happened yesterday and I am sure I will never forget it. I had no idea that sex even existed at that time of my life. I never would have thought that the monster in my life would turn out to be my own father. I lived in fear because of this man who I believed I could trust in all of my young life up until that night.

I remembered that very first night clearly. It was on the weekend, and my father of course, was drunk at the time. He had invited his friend Joe and his wife Barb over for a visit. This friend Joe of his was also a drunk. My father talked my mother and his friend's wife Barb into going out to play bingo.

I'm positive that my mother would have been happy to get away from him for a while, as he was already drunk at that time. My two older brothers and I were in bed already but I woke up because I had to go to the bathroom. I went to the bathroom, and then I wanted to go into the kitchen to get a drink because my throat was dry.

As I headed for the kitchen, I had to pass by the living room. My two brothers were asleep behind the closed door of their bedroom. While I was walking towards the living room, I could hear my father talking to his friend. I hung back in the hallway, listening to what they were saying. The television was on loud, tuned in to the hockey game. Of course, everyone knows how curious children are, and well, I was no exception to the rule. I also loved to talk and be with my daddy. So I called out to my father and asked "May I go get a drink in the kitchen?" He said "Sure!" so I went through the living room to get into the kitchen.

As I entered the living room, I realized I recognized the person, as he and his wife had been over many times before. I remembered that they always use to bring a big round tin container of potato chips. I said "Hello!" and asked "Dad, where did mom go?" and I was told that my mother had gone to bingo. I didn't think anything about it at that time, as she always liked to go when she could. She could not go very often so, when the opportunity came up she would go.

As I walked into the kitchen to get my drink, I could hear my father and his friend Joe talking but I couldn't quite hear what they were saying. I got my drink and then my father and Joe entered the kitchen. They began talking to me but for some reason I felt a little uncomfortable.

I didn't understand some of the things they were saying but I felt that they were words that I should have not been hearing. I decided it was time to go back to bed. Then my father said to me "Why don't you stay up for a little while? Your mother won't be home for awhile, don't worry I won't tell her you stayed up late." This is where the nightmare all began. I wasn't sure what to say but I didn't think I had much of a choice. Then my father picked me up and placed me on the kitchen table. I remember them asking me "Can you keep a secret?" I said "Yes?" I was feeling very confused and a little fearful. Then, out of nowhere, these two men became monsters. Joe put one of his hands over my mouth and the other one around my stomach and held me down on my back on the kitchen table. My father, who had a hold of my legs, pulled my long nightgown up, yanked off my panties and threw them to the floor.

I was never so afraid in my young life as that night and I began kicking and I tried to scream but I couldn't because of the hand over my mouth. The tears were streaming down my face, and they didn't care. They had something in mind and they weren't going to stop until they got whatever it was that they wanted.

My father kept on saying "Don't worry we aren't going to hurt you." However, they already were so I wasn't about to believe them. My father unzipped his pants as he spread my legs apart. He then tried several times to enter me, having difficulty because of my size. When he finally did, I was in horrific pain and thought there can be nothing worse than this. Shock wasn't the word for what I was feeling, as it was the most terrifying experience I had ever had. I really began to squirm and kick to break free from the terrible place I was. Then my father got mad and said "Shut up or you're really going to get it!" My own father, hurting and touching me was now threatening me too. What could get worse than that? This was too much for me and I felt like I had to get out. I remember thinking to myself over and over that; I just had to get away.

All of a sudden, it was as if I got away and I ran to the fridge. Somehow, I ended up on top of the fridge trying to hide so they couldn't get me. I thought they couldn't come up and get me, and I would be safe. Now I thought I could scream loud enough to wake my brothers. However, before I could, I heard my father was talking as if I was still on the table. I had my head facing the wall. As I slowly turned around, I couldn't believe what I saw. I looked toward the table as I sat on the fridge and I watched my father and his friend raping this little girl. I couldn't believe my eyes. There lay this child, still wearing her nightgown of white flowers on a light pink background crying and trying to fight for her life to get away from these monsters. I saw the fear in her big dark brown eyes, her long hair a tangled mess. Then, as I watched them hurt her, I realized that this scared little girl was me. I didn't know what happened but I was in two places at the same time. I watched them touch me all over my body like animals. I know that my father did not ejaculate in me that night because I watched sperm come out of his penis and end up all over my stomach. I never felt so sick and disgusted in my life.

I remember after they were finished with me my father threatened my life and said "This is your fault! Don't you dare tell anyone about this, and if you do tell anyone you'll be sorry!" He then said "Well even if you do tell anyone no one will ever believe you over me." "Everyone will hate you for lying and we will send you away to a place for bad girls, and you will never see your family or friends ever again." Then, he said "Get cleaned up and get the hell to bed!" I watched myself jump off the table crying my heart out as I ran to the bathroom. I turned on the faucet, washing my body and noticed that my "private area" was covered in blood.

It hurt to wash and the bleeding didn't seem to stop. I didn't know what to do! I never saw blood there before. How was I going to find a bandage for this? I grabbed a large handful of toilet paper to soak up the blood and left the wad of paper there as I pulled my panties back up. Looking up in the mirror, I barely recognized myself. My eyes were swollen and my face red and tear stained. I washed my face and hands. I felt pain just about everywhere, and then went to bed.

I didn't know how I ended up back inside my body but I did, I guess. I didn't sleep that night at all but instead I cried silently until I heard my mother come home. Then later, I heard their friends finally left and my parents went to bed. I spent well over half the night trying to think about how to act when I got up in the morning so that no one could tell what I had gone through. I tried to remember how I acted before this. It was as if I was a totally different person. I thought "Well, I was always happy in the morning and all day long." I practiced acting like that a few times in my head. From that night on, I truly believed that my father was no other than the devil himself. For when he first looked into my eyes that very first minute I knew he was evil. He had to be the devil because I never thought that my own father would ever get enjoyment out of hurting his only daughter. I know that he knew how badly he hurt me but he didn't care at all. I made my first belief right then - so much for thinking that parents love their children - it's not always true. From that day on, I thought that my father hated me.

The next day, when I got up, I knew I had to be in a good mood. My father greeted me with a threatening look. His eyes changed to the same evil stare from the night before and I knew I had to keep my mouth shut. The look of his eyes terrified me to my very core, as it was like looking into the very soul of the devil. I flashed back to the bathroom, seeing my reflection in the mirror as I was cleaning up and saw the same dark brown eyes that I shared with my dad. I saw the dark angry evil look in my own eyes, and from that day on, I had another belief, that I was the devil's daughter. The rest of the day, my father treated me as if nothing had ever happened. When I went into my room later on, I found money that I knew I didn't have before. I knew it must have been to keep my mouth shut but I couldn't understand why he told me it was entirely my fault and that I would be the one in trouble.

Later that day, our whole family drove to the city to pick up our grandma, my father's mother. She would join us for Sunday dinner as this was a weekly event. She was in the hospital paralyzed from the neck down from MS-Multiple Sclerosis and was like this since her early twenties. I looked forward to these visits because I enjoyed helping her with eating her meal and holding her lit cigarette to her mouth. That day however, changed that, for when I looked into my grandma's eyes, I saw the same dark evil look.

That night, as I lay in bed, all I could think about was

whether my father would come after me. In addition, I also thought of whether I would end up in the "Bad girls place" or not. In my mind, I thought they would beat me and treat me much worse than what my father was doing to me. What about my mother and my brothers? Would I never get to see them again? This was a huge worry for me, especially with my mother. As I lay there still in so much pain from the night before, all I could think of is was this going to happen to me again or was that the only time? I was still afraid to sleep and I was frightened for my life and being taken away from my family. I did not know what to do. I couldn't tell my mother that it hurt so bad to go to the bathroom along with my insides. I knew I had to deal with this all on my own with no one to talk to about anything that had happened to me. I was so scared and alone, the only thing that I could do was cry silently clinging to my teddy bear for protection and love that I could not get from anyone.

The rest of the week went by as usual. I went to school, trying to act normal and not saying anything to anyone, even though I still felt the pain in my private area. That Friday night however, my father arranged for my mother to go out with my aunt to play bingo. Again, my nightmare started. I was in bed when he came into my room. I knew I could not scream, so once again I "left" my body. Once again, I saw a little girl being sexually abused by her evil father. He did things no man should ever do to a child. Later in the bathroom cleaning up, I saw those eyes, and after that, I was too afraid to look at my own eyes again.

From the very first night, I could never stand the smell of rum as he always drank rum and coke. It always made me feel sick inside and still does after all these years. After that night, I believe that I never was truly close to many people as I was afraid of what might happen. I really can't remember being close to my family as in kissing my parents goodnight or I would kiss my mother but I recall being too frightened to kiss my father.

He began molesting me every weekend until one night he came into my room during the week, even though my mother was in the next room sleeping soundly. I could smell rum on his breath, and instantly was scared. I knew what he wanted even though it wasn't the weekend.

When he was done with me, he threatened me, saying he would actually kill me if I said anything at all. Again, I found money, this time it was in my little purse that I kept hanging in the closet. He must have put the money in then I was in the bathroom cleaning my abused body. I always thought that the monsters were under the bed or in the closet. Then it hit me that monsters are real but they are not supposed to be the people in your life that you trust. They say there is a god, but right then, I believed that there couldn't be a god for a god would never let anything happen to an innocent child. My father would say jump and I was too frightened to do anything but say how high. I had to do the most sickening sexual acts in my life.

I started school that year and I had two friends in the apartment building that we lived in. One of my friends names were Kim and the other one was Sara. I remember how I would bug my mother into either letting me stay overnight at one of their houses or for one of them to stay at our house at night so I always had a bit of safety. Even on school nights, we usually were allowed to have them over, as my parents were friends with their parents. I thought for sure that if I had a friend over that nothing could possibly happen. As I got a little older I seemed to be able to leave my body any time I wanted. I practiced all the time so this gave me a way to get away whenever I had to. This I believe helped me a lot as the years went by.

As my father continued his unbearable behavior, he started using me as a sex object for himself and also his friends. I still can't understand how all these men did things to me. I soon became more frightened of all of them, and I began to think all men must be the same way. They never ever seemed to care how I felt. They must not have ever felt guilty. I always felt sick, dirty and ashamed when they started to molest not only me but my friends too. I was so young that I just wanted them to leave me alone but I will never forgive myself for the things that I let happen to my friends. For this, I will always be truly sorry. At the time I was so scared of what they were doing to me that I never thought about the pain that they were going through also. The only thing that I thank God for is that at least they could go home whenever they wanted.

I tried to stay at my friend's house as often as possible. This seemed to work for a while, and I thought I had outsmarted him, and he couldn't hurt me. As I believed that my father was the devil, I started to think that, because I was able to leave my body whenever I wanted, there must have been the same darkness in me, also. At one time, I thought that I had to stay and watch my father and his friends molest me but then I began to leave the house so I never had to watch anymore. It wasn't until I began to see other spirits in my traveling that it really made me wonder if they were dead or if they were just like me.

It wasn't until after my grandmother died that I realized that what I was seeing were spirits, not always people leaving their body. I must say how frightening that was! Also, being raped was a lot worse than the spirits at least they never hurt me at all.

From the very first night I was molested, I am sure I never had a peaceful night sleep since. After that night, I couldn't believe how many times my father molested me. I couldn't count even if I wanted to. It didn't take long before my body and mind were numb. I didn't feel like I really existed. Even though my nerves were shot, I still carried on the best I could. Some people block out everything but I always knew exactly what he was doing even if I did jump out of my body or not. When I returned to my body, I could feel everything that had happened. Even if my soul was gone, I always knew what he did to me.

Then my father began entering my room at night during the week. I'm not sure if he began drinking vodka then so I wouldn't have been able to smell it. Nevertheless, I know it was during the week that he started drinking vodka.

As I said before, I tried to have friends over to spend the night with me so my father would stay away. I know now that it was such a bad mistake. I was young and was only trying to protect myself. I feel now I could have damaged their lives and feelings towards men and, for this, I am truly sorry. If I could take everything back and change the past, I would change everything without a second thought. There is one thing that I am grateful for and that is when my friends were over I knew that my father and his friends did not attack my friends the way they attacked me. They only did very minor things to them as they were afraid that they would tell their parents. This I did know for a fact. My father and his friends mainly just flirted with my friends even though that was wrong and they likely frightened them, at least they were never molested like I was. I am very happy to say that at least even though it was never fair for them to go through that and I wish that I had never put them at risk like I did and for that I am sorry.

2

The Secret is Revealed

One night drunk as usual, he came to me when I had my friend over for the night. My mother was at bingo and I thought I would be safe with a sleep over. He came into my room after we had fallen asleep and began to molest my friend. He covered her mouth with his hand while threatening my friend. Immediately I pleaded and begged him to stop, but he did not listen. He put his hand down her panties and tried to put his finger in her. Something made him stop, but not before he left her frightened and of course crying. Too afraid to go home, she laid there quietly sobbing, and I held her in my arms, crying together until we fell asleep.

The next morning, she went home, and told her parents what he had done to her. They lived in the same building as we did and they were good friends with my parents. Once they had found out what my father had done to their daughter, they phoned the police to have him charged with molesting children.

When the police arrived, they questioned her. She told them what he had done to her, and that he was doing it to me. After they talked to her, they came to talk to me. I thought for sure they were going to take me away, like my father said, but he was wrong. They took me to a separate room and began to question me. I did not know what to say as my father threatened me so many times as he molested me.

They began to ask me things that I really did not want to answer. I was only nine years old at the time and I was so petrified that they were going to take me away that I did the only thing I could think of. I lied to them. It was easy after all I had been living in a lie for the last four years. I told the police a couple of stories about some of the things he had done to me. I did tell them that he put his hands down the front of my pants and little things like that. I never ever told them the really awful things; I was too frightened to find out what my father would do to me after they left. I thought he would kill me for sure.

So even though I knew it was wrong to lie, I felt like I had no other choice. At any rate he was charged twice that day, one for my friend and one for me. The police took him down to the police station. I thought they were going to keep him in jail but they didn't. He came home late that night.

I remember how afraid I was when he walked into the house. He just gave me that look and it did not take me very long to go to my room and stay there the rest of the night. All that went through my head was that he had gotten in trouble with the police. He had always told me that I would be the one to get into trouble but I didn't, it was his fault, not mine. I was relieved to know that.

The next day I got up early to get ready for school. I must admit that I was frightened to go to school. I knew my friend would be there. I thought that she would say something to everyone but she did not. I apologized to her and we talked just a little bit about what had happened. I told her that we had to move away and she told me that she also was moving away. I told her that we had to move in ten days. We played together until moving day.

We only moved about two blocks away but I still had to go to a different school and make new friends. That seemed easy to me, as I was always very friendly. We moved into a townhouse complex and many children there were my age. It was not very long before I had made lots of new friends. My father seemed to leave me alone since the police had arrested him. So I thought that, it was the end of that problem in my life. It also made me understand that not everyone's father abused them. I have to say that at that time I did believe that my father was the devil and he was the only one who would do these things.

I still cannot ever recall anyone in the family saying anything to me that night but I am sure that no one had any idea of what he was doing to my friends or me. He was charged but only in family court. He only got two years probation, along with no alcohol for one year.

My mother had no idea of any of this. She was as afraid of him as much as the rest of us and we could not leave because there was nowhere to go. The only place we could have ever gone would have been his father's house. My father had an abusive way about himself that not many people knew about or cared to know about, for that matter. I think that most people don't truly care unless they have to actually live it every day as we all did. He never would have let us leave, anyway.

We also had no money to leave with, not for my mother and us three children. Even if we all had of went to my grandfather's house my father would not leave us alone no matter what.

After we all moved out, everyone thought he had left me alone and he did, but it did not take him very long to get back to his old true self again. I know that everyone had thought that he had left me alone after being charged but they were very much mistaken. My father did not obey the law as he began drinking again not long after we moved. I recall how he started to take me to his work sometimes and on the way, in the car; he always molested me and made me do things that I surely never wanted any part of. Everyone at his work seemed to like me and a lot of the people would give me money to spend on candy. They were all very nice to me but I always felt odd about taking the money they would give me as I thought that eventually they would expect me to do something in return, as most of them were men.

My father started getting me to drink with him and I found myself being able to drink a lot after a while. I did this so I would not have to think too much about what he was doing to me. This of course was only when my mother was out. When she would come home, she knew I was drunk but he would give her some lame excuse like I asked him if I could try it or something stupid like that. I knew she was too afraid to say much as he would have gotten really mad and none of us wanted to go through that so she kept silent for all our sake. For that, I never blamed her in the least. It just seemed a lot better if I was numb everywhere when he molested me. That was the only way to cope was if I was numb.

As time had passed I thought that there had to be a catch to him taking me to his work and as it turned out, I was right. The money that a lot of them gave me left me feeling that something did not feel right about them. They did start coming over to the house, most of the time it was only on the weekends. I always tried my hardest to go to my friends but he was too smart to let me get away. He and his friends would get drunk and they would bring their wives to keep my mother busy. They usually went out to bingo. I on the other hand would be stuck with the men and my mother would think that I had gone to my friends.

They would get me drunk as well, and then they would make me watch dirty movies with them.

I never saw anything so disgusting in my life. The things the people would do were unbelievable. Then without any remorse, my own father would take pleasure in letting his friends rape his only daughter. I had never in my life felt so dirty, cheap, abused and used like a toy you would buy from the store then smash into a million pieces. I never in my life could ever think of anyone doing something like this to their own children. Not all of his friends molested me. There were a few nice ones. It is truly amazing that my own father had the nerve to let so many men molest me and just stand by and watch it happen. It got to the point that I never, ever wanted to be at home.

I was a bundle of nerves. My hands always would shake and if anyone asked me, I would just say that most of our family did the same thing. I cannot believe that for such a young girl I must have been very strong willed for I seemed to handle things pretty well or maybe I was just too frightened so I pretended it never ever happened. However, when I was being molested I had never felt so weak and helpless in my whole life. It was really hard to deal with the guilt I felt.

Then my father had begun to invite my friends to spend the night. We were about eleven or twelve by this time. When they did spend the night they were offered a drink or two and they thought that was just great at the time. They did not mind my dad and his friends flirting with them but I was sure that they did not think that they would be raped once they got drunk. At first, they did not have any thing happen to them and for that, I was relieved. But I knew what was about to happen, so I tried to get them to do different things like going to the mall. This worked for a while but my father did whatever it took to con them back. He was always giving us all money or ordering pizza for us so they loved to stay at my house, their parents did not let them do that many things. They thought he was the greatest father ever. Little did they know that he was the devil playing tricks on them – until he could get what he wanted from them.

Then one night he and his friends finally made their move. At first they just did little things to them like grabbing their breasts jokingly to see if they seemed to mind or not. I myself was surprised that they did not seem to mind at all. I could not understand this so I assumed it must have been the alcohol. They did however keep coming back for more. I never thought that I would have believed this if it were not for the fact that I witnessed this for myself. I did not know what to do or say for that matter, so I did the cowardly thing, nothing.

I was never sure what my dad and his friends did to my friends but I do know that they always wanted to stay at my house. I do however remember this one time we found a pair of panties that did not belong to me in the hallway closet and I thought for sure that they did actually belong to one of my friends. I am very positive that they were also molested. For a fact, many of my friends did have to go through some of the same things that I had to. Then I think to myself that I could have never let any of it happen to them if I had not been so afraid of what was happening to me. I still wonder to this day if they ever got over it or if they ended up in therapy as I did years later. For I will never forgive myself for what they went through, I am truly sorry, but at that time in my life I was too young to realize what I was doing to my friends. I wish none of this had ever happened but I cannot turn back time and change everything that my father and his friends had done to them.

I pray that they never suffered the way that I did. By this time, I was only about twelve years old and I wished that I had been old enough to move out on my own. Mind you, that it had just been a pipe dream of mine that would not come true for many years yet. My father had heart trouble and our whole family did in fact wish that he would end up either in the hospital or that he would even die so we could get rid of him once and for all. He did begin to kick us out of the house as the abuse got worse. He got off early on Friday's so I remember how frightened we were to come home from school.

He would be at home drunk as usual just waiting to start a fight and we knew we would end up either kicked out of the house or if it was a really big fight, then the police would show up and do nothing, and we would end up on the street either way.

We would go to my grandfather's house but that was his father, he would always cause even more trouble. There were so many times that I was at my grandfathers and went out to be with my friends and my dad would follow me everywhere I went. I was so frightened that I would run into any apartment complex or the mall that was close by. As I ran, he would be yelling to me saying "Your my daughter and no matter what you do or where you go, I will find you. You will never get away from me for very long." I was so frightened that I could have died right there and then.

This one night when I was still twelve, I remember my father coming into my room at about two o'clock in the morning. I lay there petrified and not knowing what to do. Well I had to have done something to make him mad and yell and scream at me. I know that I had on a long nightgown because he had ripped it right up the one whole side. The next thing I can remember is that he had woke everyone up and I was forced to leave. It was winter and he was not going to let me change my clothes. My mother had begged him to let me change my clothes and he finally agreed. Not one of them knew what had happened and everyone was too afraid to ask, and he would have just lied anyway. My grandfather lived two to three blocks away from us and I was in a state of panic as I began to walk. My father would not allow anyone else to go with me so I had to go on my own. It was so cold and dark outside and I was always so short that my jeans were always too long. As I walked to my grandfather's house my pants dragged along the ground. It was so quiet that I could have sworn that someone was following me the whole way there. I kept looking behind me the whole way there. When I finally got there I had noticed that everyone was up and waiting for me. My mother had called them to tell them that I was on my way there. I was so relieved once I got there and I had cried the whole way. Once I had entered their house they called my mother to tell her that I had made it their safely.

The first thing that they did once I was settled inside was ask me "what happened?" I told them that he must have been in a bad mood or something and that I was awake so he took it out on me. I was shaking with fear as I always did. I will never forget the next thing that happened. There was a bang on the door and my grandfather told me, my cousin Ellie, and my one aunt Michelle to get upstairs. The three of us ran up the stairs scared to death that he was going to come after us. My other aunt Sheila, my older cousin Dwayne and my grandfather were still downstairs waiting to greet my father. My other aunt, my younger cousin (who must have only been about seven years old at the time) and I sat on the bed in the bedroom huddled together in fear that he was going to come up after us.

All that we could here was my dad yelling for me saying "Cheryl, get downstairs right now!" The aunt that was upstairs with me would not allow that and she grabbed a hold of my arm and told me to stay with her. So of course I did, as I was too afraid to go downstairs anyway. My grandfather and other aunt were trying to reason with my father but that was always impossible as for whatever he said went. No one could ever change his mind, as he was always right of course.

We began to hear things, breaking. We heard the coffee table being thrown. That is when my grandfather had, had enough. All of a sudden, we could hear a struggle and the next thing we heard was a commotion outside. We ran to the bedroom window to see what was happening. It was then that we saw my grandfather beating up my father. They were rolling in the snow and my father was finally being beaten up. That made me feel so good and when it was over my grandfather threw my screaming father in the car and told him that I was staying with him and to get lost. As my father drove away, we all felt a big sigh of relief come over us.

When we went downstairs, we noticed that the coffee table had been broken and saw the things that my father had thrown around the living room. We sat there and laughed at the look on my father's face as he drove away. I stayed there for about four weeks that time. I was so happy and it was not long before my father got mad at my mother and brothers, and they ended up there also. We always enjoyed staying there as it was a nice break for a while until we ended up back at home again.

Not only did we end at my grandfathers on a regular basis, but we would also stay at our friend's house now and then. One time on a Saturday my father stayed home and the rest of us went shopping for Christmas presents. He did not seem like he wanted to come with us and it was getting closer to Christmas so we went ourselves. When we got everything done we went home. But to our surprise, our father had had all of the locks changed on the doors. Well, we did the only thing we could do we left and went to my grandfather's. It was somewhat funny because the people that lived next door did not know what had happened to us, they did not hear the usual fights. Well it was around ten thirty in the morning when we got back from shopping and no one saw us around the house.

They did however see our dog left outside in the cold all day and night, which was very uncommon. The next-door neighbors thought for sure that my father had done something to us as they were good friends of ours and knew just what he was like. Due to the fact that my father had on purpose left the dog outside all that time did not sit well with them. After that, they really thought that my father had murdered all of us and cut us into pieces and thrown us in the freezer. They called the police and told them that, and because the police were used to coming to our house due to domestic violence they believed them. The police showed up, about three or four of them and asked him what he did with us. He did not know what hit him. He just said, "I do not know where they went." The police searched the whole house including the freezer. None of us were there. This happened about three weeks before Christmas. Then just a few days before Christmas, he begged us to come home and eventually we did. Mind you, it was just to spend Christmas with the whole family, which we enjoyed so much.

I will never forget this one time. My father was home early as it was a Friday. As usual he was drunk by the time we got home from school. We waited for my mother to get home from work as we did many Fridays. When she came home, we would all go in together. When we entered the house, everything seemed fine for the time being. My older brother Willy who was five years older than me was out of school by this time and worked as a printer full time.

My other brother Danny, who is about a year and a half older than me, was still in school along with myself. We also worked part time after supper and on weekends at the same printing company as our older brother. Our uncle James owned this company and my brothers and I had worked there since I was twelve years old. Not only did this give us extra money but also it kept us out of the house at night, which was a relief. We also had a lot of our friends work there. My uncle needed a lot of help at the time. We worked most nights along with the weekends. We had lots of fun there.

By this time, I had just turned fourteen. My father was still molesting me without my family's knowledge. Only four of my closest friends knew about this and they never told my secrets, for that alone I was grateful. My oldest brother Willy was going out with one of my best friends, Lorrie. She was two years older than I was. She is still my best friend to this day. She worked and lived with us. My other brother Danny was also going out with another one of my best friends, Janny who is also still my best friend to this day. I started hanging around with them from the time I was eleven. They are in the dedications at the beginning of my book. They both live far away from each other but we always keep in touch. I thank God that they were not the ones who were victims of my father's handy work, even though they had to walk on eggshells for many years as we all did. They went through a lot of fights with our father but they never turned their back on us at all. I love and consider them both as my sisters as I was the only girl. They are still my sisters and will remain that way for the rest of my life.

Anyway, there was this one night we thought it was going to be a peaceful night. But it just did not turn out that way. As my father became drunker, the fights resurfaced as usual. Willy's girlfriend Lorrie had just finished a load of laundry, folded it and placed it in the laundry basket. She had left it in the basket and put it on the bed just for a few moments until she had time to put it away. Well my father was a clean fanatic and that was all it took to set my father off. We had a Recreational room in the basement and my brother Willy kept a lot of his records and stereo system down there. He also had a drum set that he played down there in the basement. Most of his friends also played different instruments and they all would practice down there. My mother worked at a record company and she got five free records a month. We all took turns getting our own records. Needless to say, my brother Willy would usually get us to pick the records that he liked and they would usually end up in his collection. We did not mind that at all for he was the collector not us. This was where he lost his temper that night.

It never took much to make my father mad and that basket of laundry that was not put away was all it took. So for spite he went down to the Recreation room and threw my brother's stereo across the room. He also broke many of his records, all while my brother was in the shower. When he got out of the shower, he heard this big commotion.

He went downstairs and found out what my father did to his things. He was so furious that he grabbed his coat and stormed out of the house. He went around to the back door and got on his motorcycle. We had glass doors at the back of the house. He started up his motorcycle and drove away. Then all of a sudden, I saw him coming towards the back sliding glass doors. I thought that he would begin to slow down but I was sadly mistaken instead he sped up and drove his motorcycle right through the one closed sliding door. The shattered glass went everywhere. I was sitting in the living room on a lounge chair directly across from the sliding doors. The glass flew right at me and one big sharp piece just missed me by about an inch. Then my brother pulled his bike out of the window and parked it. He took the key out and stormed into the house he came after my father.

That's when all hell broke loose. My brother went into the kitchen, grabbed my father's bottle of rum and began to pour it down the drain. My father was so furious that he came right after my brother. It would not have been a fair fight as my father had heart problems and my brother wanted revenge. The only difference was that my father grabbed a butcher's knife from the kitchen knife rack. We called the police and when they came my father still had the knife in his hand. He said, "I'm going to stab that police officer right in the back when he walks through that door." He did chicken out though and when they came, he had the knife behind his back, but as soon as they turned their backs he threw it in the kitchen sink. I thought for sure that they were going to charge my brother for breaking the glass door but when they saw what my father had done to my brother's stuff, they said that he deserved it. We laughed, they were right he did deserve it after all he had done. Needless to say, we were kicked out of the house, but what else was new?

This other time it was Friday the 13th and I remember that it turned out bad for us for some reason and he always blamed it on us. Any way, he was mad at all of us and a big fight broke out. He and I got into an argument and he grabbed a frying pan and began trying to hit me with it. I did not know what to do so I grabbed a great big pitchfork to try to do the only thing that I could and that was to protect myself. My older brother grabbed the frying pan from my father and he told me to put the pitchfork down, I didn't want to but I did it anyway. I can still remember all the yelling and with my brothers, there for protection I could have said whatever I wanted for my protection. Then my father said to me that I have always hated him anyway and I was mad at him all these years. To this I said the only thing that I could. I told him that he was absolutely right. I did hate him. Then I asked him "How could you blame me for that after everything that you have done to us?" Well, that did not sit well with him as he charged at me and grabbed my jeans and completely ripped the whole one side of them right up to the top. Then he grabbed hold of me and threw me out the door. One of our neighbors was walking by at the time and when he threw me, I landed right into my neighbor's arms. He was a bit surprised but he did not mind it much as long as I was okay. Mind you, it was not very often that anyone did anything as he made most of our neighbors worried of what he might do next.

Needless to say, we were all kicked out of the house that night as well. I never could understand why Friday the 13th was always a nightmare for us. We always came home to a fight and it always ended up with us out on the street.

My father did have heart trouble but he also played on it a lot. He sometimes acted as if he was having a heart attack when he was actually fine. One night he was in the upstairs bathroom already in a bad mood and was mad at my brother Willy as usual. Well he decided that he was going to act as if he was having a heart attack when he was actually faking the whole time. Then we heard something smash from upstairs. My brother Willy had said some smart remark as my father was on his way down the stairs. Well for someone having a heart attack he sure could run down the stairs after my brother pretty darn fast.

He made a big mistake in going after my brother that time, as he was already very upset with him. As my father began to grab my brother, I knew my brother was ready for him this time. In a split second, my brother took a hold of my father and began to choke him. I can honestly say that as we watched my father being choked and turning blue I just wanted my brother to kill him. I actually prayed for it to happen as I figured that he deserved it for all the pain and suffering that he put all of us through over the years. Then all I could hear was my mother saying "Don't do it. Don't do it!" "He isn't worth going to jail over." My other brother Danny and both of their girlfriends tried to get my brother off my father until they finally succeeded. I was disappointed at the time. But then again I didn't want my brother spending the rest of his life in jail over an idiot like that. Needless to say, we all ended up on the street.

After a while not only did he play on his heart, but he also began trying to commit suicide. He would slice his wrists but never in the right spot and never quite deep enough. One time he even tried to hang himself but he was too afraid to kick the chair that he was standing on out from under himself. Then we thought, "Let's see if we can get him into the hospital for observation." But he was the only one that could do that. Therefore, that did not work for us at all. Then we got wise to his games so every time he said that he was having chest pains we would just call an ambulance. We knew that if an ambulance was called, they would have to take him to the hospital and it worked. But because he liked the attention so much, he actually complained about his heart more often. When it was heart related, they had to keep him in the hospital for seven to ten days. That was the happiest time for us as there was no stress at home for at least a week or more.

A few months before my sixteenth birthday my father tried to molest me for the very last time. It was the middle of the night and he came into my room with just his underwear on. I had finally found enough courage and I screamed very loudly. My brother Danny and my mother were the only ones home at the time. My father was not only surprised but I think that he was actually frightened. He ran into his and my mother's bedroom which had a bathroom in it, and he grabbed a towel and wrapped it around himself. Then he said loudly "What's going on." My mother and brother woke up and came running into my bedroom. They said, "What's wrong?" The only thing that I could tell them was "Dad would not leave me alone and that he wanted me to have sex with him." My brother asked me "Are you just having a bad dream?" "No I'm not having a bad dream." I told my brother and mother and when I told them, I knew that they believed me. A big argument broke out between my parents and of course, we were kicked out eventually. Even after that night, I never told my mother what had gone on between my father and me in the past or that he had ever done anything to me at all. My mother still had no idea that anything had happened to me, even though my father had already been charged with molesting several children by that time. All the children in the past that he had been charged with, and he still always managed to get away with it. I never thought that he would ever get any jail time for what he had done. After that night, I stayed away from home for almost three months. Then he begged my mother to talk to me and convince me to come home. They were even going to put a lock on my bedroom door just to make sure that he would leave me alone.

Eventually, I finally did come home but this time I was different. I walked into my room as my father told me that there was a surprise for me. He and my mother had redone my bedroom. I guess that was his way of telling me he was sorry for what he did to me. He never told or showed us that he loved us other than buying us off with something he knew we wanted. That day that I came home, I knew that this would be the last time he ever laid his grubby hands on me again.

I had already been on nerve pills for just over a year and a half. One thing that I could not understand is that once I turned sixteen and went to the doctors for a physical, they did many tests and found out that my insides had been damaged due to my father. My father went to the same doctors and they knew about the charges that he had gotten and they still never did anything about what he had done to me. I still do not understand why the doctors could not do anything but they never did. They told me that my father had pushed my insides up so far inside me and that my bowels were like tissue paper. After I found that out, they said "Chances are, you may never have children." I could have killed him. I figured that he had already taken away my childhood and now maybe the rest of what I wanted later on in my life. More than anything else I wanted to have a child. I couldn't even begin to wonder what my life would end up like without a child in it. This was one of my lifelong dreams and now the thought of it never being able to happen ate away at me for many years. I always worried about my father getting me pregnant as I started my period when I was only eleven. I now knew that I was worried for nothing.

I felt nothing but hate for my father. I figured that he had already ruined my life thus far and now he had damaged me for good. I just wanted him dead I was no longer afraid of him. If he made me mad, I would just start screaming and yelling at him at the top of my lungs until I had nothing left inside me to give. I always spent my life worrying about what he would do to me and now I didn't care at all. Revenge was what I wanted and that was all. I never wanted to be alone in any room of the house or car with him because I always worried in the past what he would do to me. Now he made me feel sick to my stomach just to look at him. That's what kept me going I think, it was pure hate for that stranger that no one really knew. Whatever he did, nobody ever knew the truth about him or what went through his evil sick mind. Not anyone! I thought that I knew what was in his mind for I was the one that he damaged for life. I knew that he had to have hated me from the day I was born.

I didn't know how to cope with my feelings so I just kept them bottled up inside me for all those years. I thought I was going crazy most of the time but I kept myself sane by writing everything down in a book. I wrote down every single thing that he had ever done to me. I never ever would read anything I wrote after I had written it down, I couldn't have handled reading it again. My book was so thick but I would just keep adding pages to the back of it. I always hid my book under my top mattress up near where the top of my head would lay.

Then this one Friday, I was in my room and I wanted to add something to it. When I went to get it, it was gone. I was so frightened and I knew that there was no way that I could ask anyone if they knew what happened to it, so I said nothing.

When I finally had enough courage to go downstairs, I looked at my father first and boy, did I ever get a dirty look. Then I knew for sure that he was the one who had taken it. I knew right then, that was the last time I could ever do anything like that again. I had spent years writing in that book. All my fears and feelings over the years were gone and I felt like part of my life was dead. I didn't know what I was going to do now. That was my release and how I coped with what was going on in my life.

Then, I figured out another way to express my inner feelings. I began writing my father letters on how he made me feel. I knew I couldn't tell anyone so that was my escape. Now that I was wise towards my father and I knew that he was searching my room to see what was in there. I would just write the letters and then I would burn them up. This way I got my feelings out and there was never anything in my room for my sneaky father to find. I thought that he must have always been in my room looking around for anything that he could find. I had no privacy whatsoever and now I knew it for sure. He controlled my whole life and there was nothing I could do about it.

As the years past, my father had been charged with molesting so many children that I couldn't even keep count. I never understood how he managed to get off with it all the time. However if you were to get caught stealing or something like that you would be sent to jail. This just never made any sense to me at all. It just goes to show you what money and a good lawyer could do. That's what my father always did, he would spend thousands of dollars on a good lawyer and he got off almost every time. Well, sometimes he would get a fine and probation. But basically, it was just a slap on the wrist. In addition, it was just awful when you would see so many people going to jail for a lot less. Such as things like unpaid fines or theft but never for sexual abuse when that is something that really interferes with the victim's personal life.

The main reason that I wish to tell you about this is because it might help a lot of people who went through the same things in one way or another. Now that I realize what he did, I now know that there's no way this should have ever happened, especially when most of the time it is usually a family member that you trust that does something like this. However, it seems they're the people that you can't rely on. I learned not to trust anyone, especially around your own children, for no one really knows what anyone feels deep down inside.

Everyone thought my father was the greatest man you would ever want to meet. So when he told me that I was to blame for everything I thought it must be true. It wasn't until I realized that he was the one doing the raping not me. So how could it be my fault when he attempted to persuade my friends into doing things that bothered them. So, they only let my father flirt with them up to a certain point. I was there every time so I knew my father never had the chance to physically rape them.

Then he began going out for walks at night with our dog. When he returned home most of the time, it would be about two hours later. I always heard him return home, even if I was upstairs listening to music on my stereo. I still knew that something was about to happen those nights. I always recall him saying that the police were going to be coming to get him. The only thing I could never understand is why when my father had been charged that the judges never threw him in jail. He seemed to always get away with it and the courts still allow criminals to get away with it to this day. When do all the victims ever get to feel safe when nothing ever happens to their abusers? They should be put in jail instantly before they put other helpless children through this horrible experience. We are the ones that should feel safe, not them. So, believe me, it is never anything that any of the children do. The abusers are the ones who have the problems, not the innocent people that are too frightened to do anything about it. Not once did anyone ever ask me if I wanted to receive any type of counseling for what he and his friends had done to me, or anyone else that I knew of that he abused for that matter. We are the people that are doing all of the suffering while they are just getting their rocks off. I would bet that a large amount of these people either blame themselves or sometimes even end up dead. It's unbelievable that the innocent live there whole life with this and no one seems to care and the guilty truly always seem to get off. They can get all kinds of help but in reality, they just can't wait to go out and search for their next victims. After all these years, there is still no justice. The probation that most offenders get will never help what the victims have to go through.

There is one thing that I will never understand and that is that these people that have children of their own. Let's say they are grown up, one is a boy, and the other one is a girl. Then, their son was arrested for child abuse, how these parents can do everything in their power to get the charges dropped for their son. They would even pray that their son would not receive any jail time at all. I cannot understand why they would not want their child to realize what he put the girl or boy though by molesting them and take his punishment accordingly. They should also realize that they need to receive some counseling on their own because they should understand that what they had done was terribly wrong. I often wonder if their daughter was ever molested if they would just ignore it or would the parents want that person to be thrown in jail.

I have seen this happen before and I couldn't believe that the parents never wanted anyone to know what their son had done as that would always be the big family secret. On the other hand if their daughter was raped everyone in the family including their son who was already charged with rape would not only tell everyone what had happened to their daughter but be furious and want revenge on the man that raped their daughter. Does this not sound weird or what? I myself know for a act that if that was my child that I would get that child some serious help. Molesters never stop; they just get sneakier about it instead. Also, if my daughter was raped, I would get her all the help that she needed in order to try to heal from that terrible ordeal. These people are sick and that thought never leaves their mind. If you are married to someone who is a molester, the chances are that they might end up molesting your children. Let me say that your children will be afraid.

I still thank God for giving me a happy personality. I always found the strength within myself to be able to hide my true feelings. When I think of the people who never had the strength to go on and either end up running away from home and end up on the streets or torture themselves over things that they had no control over I feel bad for them. I just feel like crying as I still recall everything that my father and his friends had done to me as if it just began to happen yesterday.

When we did move into the townhouse, I prayed that everything would stop. I remember how my father received a bonus every June from work and he always bought either new furniture or a new car. He always got his bonus before school was out for the summer. We were allowed to pick anything we wanted for passing each year. My brothers always wanted a new dirt bike or bicycle but I always wanted a dog. I never could have one in the apartment so when we moved into the townhouse I finally got one. He was the most beautiful, loving type of collie I ever saw. My parents got him when he was four months old. We named him Champ and he became my best friend in the whole world. I talked to him about everything and he slept with me every night. I really began to believe that my nightmare was over but I should have known better than that.

When my father snuck into my room at night, he would just make my dog get out of my bedroom. After he had his way with me my dog waited a little while, then he would come back in with me. He was a very loving dog. As I lay there crying, Champ always jumped up on my bed and he would lie beside me as I cried myself to sleep. We would share the same pillow. I thought for sure something wasn't right, as he seemed to know what was happening to me because of the way he became afraid of my father almost instantly.

Champ's real name on his birth papers was Champlain Junior Special Twin Cedars the 2nd. His mother's name believe it or not, was Lassie. Not the real Lassie of course, but she was a show dog as Champ was supposed to be. However, we just wanted him as a pet to love and take good care of as he grew up. He did look like the real Lassie, except that he was a male instead of a female. My parents did pay a lot of money for him as he was a pure bred. Then again, my father always paid top dollar for everything, as he had to act as if he had a lot of money. He always had to have a new car every two years at least, along with new furniture all the time. He made sure that everyone thought he had lots of money. Not only did he have to show off with material things, he was a clean fanatic. We always had all the chores to do every day and we made sure we did them.

Well, getting back to my dog, he slowly grew and soon summer vacation was over and we went back to school. He figured out how to open the back sliding glass door as it was never locked so we could get in at lunch and after school. I will never forget the first time Champ opened the door, and sat down outside the school waiting for me. The principal asked, "Does anyone know whose dog is outside?" When I saw that it was my dog, I could not believe it. He began to do this every day and everyone thought he was so cute. He went up to everyone at lunch so people would pat him or maybe sneak him a snack sometimes. He became so popular that after a while everyone knew his name. The principal would even say over the intercom "Cheryl, your dog is outside waiting for you." I never thought a dog would have as many friends as he did. Champ was with us for almost fourteen years before he died. I wondered for a long time if he was going through the same thing I was, as he used to run away when my father got mad.

I still can recall how my father would get mad over just about anything. The only problem was that we would all end up getting kicked out of the house. Most of you would think that was a good thing but it wasn't at all. I remember how there was never anywhere else to go so we would always end up at my grandfather's house. This happened so many times that I couldn't even begin to fathom how many times this occurred. My father would not quit bothering us until he got his own way. My father would not quit harassing us, even when we called the police. They would always come but the only problem was that they would tell us that they did not like to get involved in domestic disputes. Then they would just give him a warning and leave. They always checked his record and they knew everything that he had been charged with but I think that if the person does not kill someone then the police cannot be bothered. This I think is the worst thing they can do as it makes people think they can get away with anything. The main point that I am trying to make is that they never knew what the innocent people had to go through after the police leave.

Things then began to go like clockwork for us. My father always got off work at noon on Friday's so we were afraid to go home after school. We usually would wait for my mother so we would not have to face him alone. Mind you, I never realized at the time but my mother was just as afraid of him as we all were. So almost every third or fourth Friday or Saturday, we would end up at Grandpa's house. And every year, around three to four weeks before Christmas, we were all kicked out. Then about a week or two before Christmas he would drive us all up the wall to come home. We did not want to but we had no other choice but to go home again. It was nice to have all the family together, there must have been at least fourteen of us and we kids had to wait until five-thirty in the morning before we could call Grandpa. The rest of the family would come over and watch us open our presents. The parents always opened their presents on Christmas Eve and the kids were only allowed to open one present each. My brothers and I were allowed to open our stockings if we woke up early, as we always did, but we had to save the rest until everyone else got there in the morning. In spite of all the problems we went through, that was the best time of the year. That was because of the whole family being together.

After Christmas was over and everything was back to what we called normal; then everything would start all over again. It seemed like we were living in circles. Every weekend was a nightmare that never seemed to go away. As we began to grow up it seemed as if things got worse, not better. My father always seemed to be causing some sort of trouble in one way or another.

I remember now how we all would wait for my mother to get home from work on Friday's before we would go home. We never knew what to expect but I now realize that we put our mother in danger more than anyone. As she was the one who always was stuck putting up with him. We would just leave and go to our friends and she was left there by herself to listen to him. Even though she married him, I know how she must have felt because we all wanted nothing more than to get away from him. I cannot believe how selfish we were to leave her alone with this man that we really never knew at all. My mother had no choice, as he treated her awfully all the time. He ordered her around as if she was a slave and at the time, none of us even realized what she was going through. For this I can say that I still feel so much regret for what we let him put her through. I am so sorry, Mom.

DEAR MOTHER OF MINE

The enormous amount of love you always give,
That has taken me many years to see.
I will never get over the love we had lost,
Because of what my father had done to me.

All the years that I must have blamed you,
For something that you did not see.
Now that I know the pain, that you went through, too,
I am truly sorry it took so long for me to see.

For if, I only knew the pain that you went through,
Then I know I would, and should, have stuck to you like glue.
I wish I could have told you what was happening to me,
As I now know that, you would have believed in me.

The evil he had brought to us all,
Seemed to have kept us all in our little shells.
As for courage, we knew nothing about,
For he definitely made sure of that.

The years I missed with you, I am beginning to remember.
The saying is true that there is no stronger love,
Than the bond that belongs to a child and mother.
I am so honored to have a mother as loving as you.

I will always love you, my dear Mother.

3

Living a Lie

The townhouse we lived in had three bedrooms. I had my own bedroom and my two brothers shared a bedroom next to mine. My parents had the big bedroom next to my brothers. I recall how much of a light sleeper I had become. I would wake up at the slightest noise that I heard. I do not recall ever sleeping right through the night without waking up quite a few times. I even began to put a nickel on the top of the bedroom door at night just so I could sleep. Every time my father came in at night, he would make the nickel fall off my door and onto the carpet. I always woke up when I heard that nickel drop. I always kept on pretending I was sound asleep but that was hard to do when you are scared to death anyway. That had never seemed to stop him as he was in my room for one reason and had decided that he would not leave until he got what he had came for.

Every time my father was charged, we had to act as if nothing had happened. We would hear his name over the radio and it was always in the newspaper. When I went to school, a lot of people would talk about it and if anyone asked us we just had to lie because we were all just so embarrassed and disgraced. Our last name was somewhat common so it was easy to act as if it was not us. Actually, there was a girl who lived less than a block away from me and she had the exact same name as I did. There was another person that had the same name as one of my brothers too. The only difference was the middle name. The only thing that was lucky for us was that we lived in a big city.

I had missed a lot of time from school from being sick and living in turmoil over what we had to deal with. We were kicked out of the house so much that I missed school a lot and keeping up with our homework was somewhat challenging when our books would be at our house and we would be somewhere else. When I was almost sixteen, I decided I did not want to go to school anymore. So I toughed it out until I turned sixteen then I finally decided that I had enough and I just quit. One of the reasons I quit also was that I had worked for my uncle since I was twelve and I got used to having money. I liked to shop and with no school left to go to, I wanted to work instead.

By the time we all had full time jobs; it was harder to get away with the lying. My one brother worked as a printer but my other brother was still in school. My uncles business had just closed down only a few months before so that left us kids without a job. I had done some babysitting for many of the neighborhood kids for quite some time. So some friends of ours offered me a full time job babysitting their two children every day. They were in school so it was mainly just before and after school. Then another woman in our townhouse complex also needed a babysitter for the same time, before and after school. The one child was dropped off at six o'clock in the morning and the other two children would be there at seven o'clock in the morning, so my day started early. My father left for work at five-forty-five in the morning so he was never there when the children arrived. They would leave our place at around five thirty to six o'clock at night usually just before my father got home from work. I would feed them their breakfast and lunch as we lived so close to the school they would come home for lunch. Then after supper at night, I also babysat two other children at night as they just lived a block and a half away. I had to baby sit them from seven at night until two o'clock in the morning. I used to take a taxicab home at night and I never got that much sleep, but I managed to do this for just over a year. During the first part of that year, my other brother who had still been in school decided to quit and also get a job. He also got a job as a printer.

Our father always said that we could quit school as long as we had jobs, so that is what we all did. When I was almost seventeen, I had finished babysitting and got a full time job at a computer company and I just loved it. I had a lot fewer hours and a lot more spare time for myself. I made more money working so I had l lot more extra money to spend. My friends and I hung around at malls a lot of the time after work and during the weekends. This way I spent a lot less time at home. My father would usually go to bed at around ten o'clock so I would come home at ten thirty or eleven o'clock just so I did not have to talk to him at all. The only thing that always bothered me was that we all had to be home for supper every day. I just hated that and even though we were older, he would still get mad if we were late or did not show up for supper. It would have caused a fight anyway so we always made sure we were there.

My parents always had a trailer and a boat so in between the summer months, we spent a lot of time camping and fishing. I loved doing those things along with the rest of our family. We've had the trailers ever since I was about seven and we always had a boat. My grandfather and the rest of our family always camped with us so that made it really nice for us all.

It seems to me that most of our problems happened in the colder time of the year. But when it got warmer, everything seemed much better. My brothers and I were always allowed to bring friends with us so we had lots of fun. My parent's friends would also come camping with us and they had a son that my older brother hung around with, so all of us were quite happy. This we did for many years. My father had a lot of holiday time in the summer so we always went camping for two to three weeks every year just to get away. Then again, we were always allowed to bring friends with us so that was great too. We usually rented cottages and left our trailer at our usual camp grounds but we would always bring our boat.

I recall how we always had so much time swimming and riding around on our mini bikes. Each year I always got my brother Danny's old mini bike and he would get my older brother Willy's. Willy would get a new one. It was like we all got a better bike each year and we had so much fun driving around on the trails. My father used to get so mad at Willy as we all had dirt bikes not road bikes. Anyway, my father as well as the rest of the campground would frequently see the police escorting Willy back to the campground, as he would always drive his bike on the main road. I recall how my father would tell him how much of an embarrassment he was because the police had brought him home.

What a joke that was! If anyone was an embarrassment to my family, it was not my brother it was my father. When I was younger, my parents always told my siblings and me to never lie. This never made any sense to me because the truth is that we spent our whole life having to live a lie. We only did it because we had to just to protect my father's reputation. I never did understand why we had to protect his reputation. It is not like he was perfect or anything. I guess he was the boss and whatever the boss said, we definitely had to obey. We were just there to bow to the master anyway. We were just his servants after all or that is how we always felt anyway. Therefore, whatever he said we did and were not allowed to ever speak our minds, we would just obey the boss. My father never tried to do anything to me at the trailer; everyone would have caught him for sure so I was usually safe for the summer. Mind you, that was only on the weekends. During the week, he did whatever he had wanted.

When we were camping, no one there ever knew what was happening to us at home. It was like living a double life all the time but that was never hard to do when we had so much practice doing this for so many years. It is so weird to be able to do this without even thinking as you would have thought that this would be a really hard thing to do. By the time I was a little bit older I always thought of how easy it would be to kill my father and get away with it as I got so used to the lying. I often thought that I could kill him and just get away with it without even blinking an eye. For that matter if any one of us killed him, I believe that we all could have lied to anyone never mind the police. I always wished that he would be killed on his way home and I often wondered if anyone of us would have even cared.

I was about fourteen, I had missed a lot of school and I always had spent a lot of time at the doctors. Not only was I already on nerve pills, which made me very tired to the point where I spent most of school time trying to stay awake and it was hard because I also had trouble with my bowels thanks to my father. I would be in crippling pain and I remember crawling on the ground so often because the pain was unbearable that I had to be taken to the hospital. My parents were never sure if it was my appendices or not, so I would always have to be taken to the hospital just to make sure. However, it was like I always said it was my bowels. I also had a lot of trouble with my periods because of my insides being pushed up so far inside of me. I had terrible cramps every month and had to be put on pills to try to help me with the pain. That never helped much and I would spend most of the week in bed. I never got over the damage that my father had done to my insides as I always had suffered for it in one way or another. Not to mention how little sleep I had gotten each night as I laid there at night wondering and worrying if my father was going to enter my room each night.

But life had to go on as I lived each day with whatever I was dealt with. When I think about it, I cannot believe that this was still going on at the age of fourteen and I was still petrified of what my father could do to me. I never thought that this would ever end. I thought about running away many times but I was even more afraid of ending up on the streets by myself at night. The thought of not knowing what trouble might arise and afraid of who might pick me up and maybe even do worse to me than what I was already going through was just too much more for me to have worried about so I stayed where I was. I always thought that it was weird that I never had heard of this happening to anyone else that I knew. Were we the only ones that had things like this happen to us? Or did I just never hear about it from anyone else? Sometimes I thought that maybe they were just too afraid to talk about it as well as I was.

It seems funny how different people go through different things. Everyone's life turns out a different way. I always thought that all of our family must have been put on this earth to suffer and I would bet that many people would have felt the same way for one reason or another. We all go through different things but it makes us stronger because of it. I always wanted my father to just be normal and leave us all alone. It was like living with a bully who always got his own way.

My mother jumped at my father's every command and he never said please or thank you. It was always "Get me this or get me that!" And I hated him for that alone. He treated her like she was his slave and she was so afraid of him that she just did whatever he said to keep peace in the family. When we had company, we were all suppose to behave and that meant to be prim and proper and never let on that anything was ever wrong. If we went visiting to friends of my parents, we had to just sit there for hours and barely talk at all. Life was a dream when we were with other people that my parents knew.

I cannot believe that I can truly say that I had forgotten I had a real mother, as I must have blocked her out of my mind. It's not like I didn't know her but I think I just must have blamed her in some way for not seeing what my Dad was doing to me. I felt like a stranger to my parents. I could not say that I loved them or just go up to them and kiss or hug them. Not ever did any of us kids do that. Years later, I asked my mother "Why, did you keep on letting my father molest me after he had been charged?" It was not until that day that I really realized that she had truly believed that, after the first time he was charged with molesting me, he had never touched me again. When I saw the look on her face that day, I did believe her with all my heart and soul. She told me that they had not slept together for years and that they did not have sex either. Well, I always knew that they slept separately but I never knew that they had not had sex in years. My mother was very shocked the day she found out that he was still sexually abusing me. After that, I spent a lot of time trying to remember as much of her as I could. I still remember things that I had forgotten about or shall I say, blocked out of my mind. I must admit he truly made us all become numb after years of torture.

One year later, when I was about fifteen years old, our dog Champ began to run away from home a lot after we had him for a little while. I thought to myself that my father was doing something to him but I could not imagine him doing something that sick. Once my father began walking Champ at night, I thought it must have been to get the kids to come over to see

Champ so he could pick a child to molest. That was such a sickening thing to do, but that wasn't the only thing he did . One day a girl that I knew very well came up to me started to tell me that she saw Champ along with my father, in the park one night.

My heart fell as I wasn't sure I wanted to hear any more, I had already suspected what she was about to say. As she began talking I felt so sick to my stomach that you could not even imagine. It was cold outside I recall it being late in the fall time. That meant that my father would have had a winter coat on and he would usually put a couple bottles of booze in his pockets. Anyway, my friend began to tell me that she, along with many of her friends, at the park and they saw my father and Champ there. She also told me that he offered them a drink. Well, they were a bit nervous of course, but she said that my father kept on bugging them. He said that no one would find out and that he had lots. So they thought about it and for sure, they were curious so they began drinking alcohol with him. She said they drank two bottles with him. That of course, was the cool thing to do. None of their parents let them do things like that. As they drank, they began to get drunk. They were having an okay time, and they did not have to be home for quite a long time so they thought my father was great. Then my father began to tell them dirty jokes so they thought that was funny. It was not until he asked them about having sex and things that began to make them wonder what he was doing.

Now the most disgusting thing of all was about to happen. I do quote my friend on this, as I thank God that I was not there to see this. My father, who I really believed loved my dog, began to undo his pants and that man literally raped my dog in front of everyone. I could have killed him and I think that if I had not been so afraid of him myself that I would have done exactly that. I was so embarrassed that I could hardly look at her. I felt so bad for my dog and now I knew for sure that my father was the most sickening and cruelest person I had ever met. Why was this man born, was it only to hurt everyone in any way that he could? Was there a reason for all of this? What did we ever do to deserve to have this man in our family? Not all of us could be bad or could we?

This I believed, he had to be the devil. I thought that no one could have been so heartless in my whole life. I finally knew that my poor dog did understand what I was going through and that's the reason he took to me so much. We both shared the same nightmare over and over again. To this day, I cannot believe that there are people out there that actually do things like that. It still makes me feel sick even until this day. All that was going through my head was how my poor dog must have felt. Then again, I figured that he must have felt the same way that I did.

Once my father did that, the kids left but she told me that my father told them that no one would believe them and he would deny everything. He said that they would get into trouble for lying in the first place. Therefore, instead of going to their parents, they just stayed away from him in the future. I knew he was the devil then, more than ever. I could leave my body whenever I wanted, along with the fact that I could see things not only ghosts. I believed that I had to be the devil's daughter. Even though I had to watch porno movies with men doing that to horses along with the awful things those women did to them. I still never thought that my own father was someone like that. I know that nothing did really surprise me when it came to my father. However I have to say that what he did really surprised me. He could have murdered someone, but this was even worse than that. I have never been as shocked in my life as I was then.

I recall my brother Willy telling me one night, while my

other brother Danny and I were sleeping, he heard my father say something to my mother that he could not believe. He said that he was in bed upstairs but he had not fallen asleep yet. As he lay there listening to my father yelling at my mother as usual, he told her something that my brother has never forgotten. As my father was yelling, he just happened to say something that made my brother more frightened then he had ever been where my father was concerned. My brother heard my father tell my Mom that he was going to go upstairs and actually kill us three kids.

My brother was so frightened that he didn't know what to do. He knew that he was the oldest and strongest of us all so he had to protect us the only way that he could, even if he wasn't sure of what he was going to do that time. He shared a bedroom with my other brother who is just over a year older than I am. My bedroom was next door to theirs. As he lay in bed panicking, he thought that he had to get up and wait for my father to come upstairs to kill us. My brother stated that my mother was crying and begging him not to hurt us but my father was too drunk to reason with. My brother got up out of bed and went out into the hallway where he spent the night. Our rooms were next door to each other, and my brother spent the night worried and waiting for my father to come upstairs to kill us. My brother left us to sleep while he stayed up all night. My brother, as well as the rest of us knew that if my father was going to do something that he usually did. He stood in the door way all night just waiting and thinking to himself that he would have to protect us even if it had meant that my brother had to kill my father or that my brother would end up dead just trying to save us.

That was not the only time he protected us from that beast. Just to think that he along with my other brother had saved my life on many occasions. There would be nothing else to say but they are both true heroes if I ever saw one. I thank them both repeatedly for everything they have ever done for me as at that time in my life, they were the only two that really understood the hell we all lived.

After a while, my parents began sleeping in the living room. My father would sleep on the couch and my mother slept on a chair that went with the living room set. He never cared that her back would kill her every day and that she went to work just the same as he did but as long as he was comfortable that was all that had mattered. I never really understood this, as they had a big master bedroom with a bathroom in it. They did this for a few years so they let me use their bedroom and for some reason my brothers still shared their bedroom instead of taking my room. I never knew why when they could have both had their own rooms but they stayed together.

My oldest brother liked to play tricks on me as I was a sucker for punishment. While I used the master bedroom, I had a bathroom also. I had collected stuffed animals for years and had owned over two hundred and fifty by this time. Well, I had owned many big stuffed animals. One was these was a Mickey Mouse animal, and it was about three and a half feet tall. My brother thought it would be funny to try to scare me with it so he hung it up in my bathroom with a rope around its neck. I had no idea what was going on and I went to bed not knowing what he had done. Thankfully, in the morning I woke up when everyone was already up. When I went into the bathroom and turned on the light, boy did I ever scream. Everyone came upstairs to see what had happened and they all laughed at me. I knew right away that it had to be my oldest brother and I could have killed him even though I thought that it was funny also.

We did have a lot of fun playing pranks on each other. We did do it a lot of times. The only problem was is that he always got the better of me. On Halloween, he always got me good. This one time he had soaped all the cars in the parking lot and it was so obvious that it was him, as his car was the only one that was untouched. I decided to get him back so I soaped his car and anyway. I didn't know this at the time as I was outside getting him back and when I came in I thought that I had got him good. However, when I had picked up my purse to go out, he took his two hands and hit my purse. When I went to get something out of my purse, it was full of broken eggs. I could have killed him. He was always one step ahead of me, and I never got the last laugh, he always got me worse then I got him.

They both feel a lot of hate for my father and I cannot say that I blame them. They also keep on trying to block out the past where as I feel that if we face what happened to us and try to understand what life is all about then maybe one day they will feel as free as I do now.

I love them both and they are both married now. My oldest brother has a wife and one daughter and my other brother has a wife and three children, one girl and two boys. I know that all of us would do anything even die, in order to save our own children. I am sure that many people say that if you never spent your life in hell as we did, then that saying is different for everyone.

I do have to say that this chapter is also for the love I always had, and always will, for my mother as her life was threatened an awful lot, too. Also to my sweetheart, Champ, my first collie but not my last as I think that they are the smartest and most caring dogs that I have ever had the privilege of owning.

May Champ who died years ago, rest in peace and let his spirit always be with me, as I know it is. For this dog, I love with all my heart and I do believe that dogs are the best friends that you can have. Champ, I still love you and always will. I now have two collies that I promise to protect to the very best of my abilities. I have done so now for all the years that I have had them and for the rest of their lives, as I love them all.

4

The Force of Evil

As the years went on, life was awful. I could not sleep. I felt like I was only put on this earth to be tortured. All the while that I was growing up after the whole family realized what my father had done to me it seemed like everyone became afraid to come near me. I felt like no one really wanted any part of me. I became the lonely outcast of the family. Sure, everyone talked to me about impersonal things or joked around but they never really were that close to me. The only people that I really connected with were my two brothers and my two best friends. The only problem was that no one ever knew exactly what had happened to me they only knew a little bit about my life. I could never tell anyone the whole story. I knew that I would never actually tell anyone some of my worst, deepest nightmares. They were too hurtful to ever talk about. I was too ashamed of myself and for what had happened. I reached a part of my life where I was numb and I often thought that how could there be a god when I was never a bad girl. My father raped me, I could not stop him. If my father was on earth to be the devil, then I was an evil child, as I could see so many things and I could not ask anyone else if they could see them or not. I never felt like I was in my body anymore. Oh sure, I know that I was around myself but always off in the distance. I felt like I was separated from my heart and my mind. Feeling numb is such a nothing sort of feeling that I cannot really even begin to describe it.

I began to hate all men as they all seemed the same. Well, I guess I cannot really say I hated all men but I had only known a few, very few, men that had never molested me. I was so sick of my father inviting men over to rape me that I felt lost, betrayed, and eventually hatred. I can remember watching porno movie after porno movie and it got to the point that I knew them all off by heart. However, the hate began to get the better of me. I was positive that there was no such thing as God, for how could God hate me that much. What did I do to deserve this? I had to be evil, I just knew it.

By the time, I had turned seventeen and had a good career in a large computer company. The younger of my two brothers and I went out and got our own place. My oldest brother had moved out a little earlier than we did. That left my mother and my father living on their own. We tried to get our mother to come with us but she stayed with my father. She did know that she could come and live with us at any time she pleased but she did not. I personally thought that she stayed with my father just to keep peace in the family. My father was still getting into trouble every now and then but my parents started spending more time going to bingo together with friends of theirs. I went with them sometimes also. I always liked bingo, and so did my parents. In the place where my brother and I lived they thought that we were married as we had the same last name and we never told anyone. The difference was we were afraid that they would think that we were too young to live on our own. Therefore, we just kept our mouth shut. We lived in a basement apartment and our windows were level with the ground.

Our father never knew where we lived, we were always afraid of what he might do so we did not tell him. When we first moved in, all we had was our sleeping bags and we had enough money for some cheap dishes and silverware. Eventually my father felt guilty and finally let us take our bedroom furniture. They bought us a pot and pan set also. Then my father decided that they were going to buy a new living room set and he let us have their old one along with the coffee tables. Eventually we bought everything that we needed. We still lived in fear, my brother always had a baseball bat near his bed, and he kept a butcher knife under his bed. I also had a butcher knife under my bed and two sets of nun chucks under my pillow just in case I needed them.

We lived together until I was almost twenty-one years old. However by then we were both living with our partners and there just was not enough room for all four of us. My brother stayed where we had been living and I had my name on a waiting list in the same town houses as my parents, I really liked it there.

Finally, someone had moved out and I was able to move in. I was only a few houses down from my parents. But now I was closer to my mother and I always had an extra bedroom just in case she needed it. My boyfriend and I did not last long, because he never wanted to work. I had been brought up to be a good worker and I just got sick of paying for him all the time. So he finally moved out. I was on my own for a while before I finally met my future husband. My father always hated all of my boyfriends but he actually really liked him. I was very surprised and happy at the same time. They hung around together all of the time along with his family. We all really liked each other and things went well for a long time.

The four of us went camping every weekend and my future husband Daniel loved to fish along with the rest of us. That's what we did. We camped and fished all weekend and I have to admit we all had a great time. My Grandfather and the rest of the family had moved over two hundred kilometers away after one of his oldest daughter had died of cancer. We were all very close to her, and her one son. My grandfather, the son of my aunt that had died, along with my grandfather's other daughter, and that aunt's daughter moved with him also. We also had a lot of other relatives that had lived near where we camped so we could see everyone. I never really liked the taste of fish but I did love to fish.

I never told my future husband Daniel about what my father had done to me as he liked to be around him and thought he was a great person. Then one time they went camping, just the two of them, my father was up to his old tricks again and my father got these two boys who were about fourteen years old to come out to the trailer with them to help do some work for some extra money. My father knew them very well so there were no problems about the kids going with him. As the day turned into night, my father got drunker and drunker. Then as he let the kids drink also so they would not realize what my father was about to do. As they, all were drinking including Daniel it was then that my father began molesting the two boys. Daniel could not believe his eyes and he got up, left the trailer, and ended up sleeping on the picnic table for the rest of the night. That happened on a Saturday night the children were supposed to be home by nine o'clock and it was already midnight.

The children's parents began to worry, so they called the camp and made my father take them home. When they finally got home, they told their parents what had happened and my father was charged not only for molesting them but also for drinking and driving. Therefore, they impounded his car and my mother and I had to drive all the way there to pick them up. Daniel did not say anything all the way home and at the time my mother and I thought that my father had just been charged with drinking and driving. We had to pick up my father's car and I drove my car home with Daniel. My mother drove my father and his car home.

On the way home, Daniel just sat there and did not say a word. I knew that something had to have happened but I just let it go for the time being. For the next few days, Daniel seemed really upset then he finally started to cry. I asked him what had happened at the trailer and he finally told the whole story. That was when I told him all about my father. He could not believe it, but he finally did when I got my oldest brother to talk to him. My brother told him all about what had happened in the past and he was shocked and had a very hard time believing it but he finally did. I was surprised that he stayed with me after knowing the truth about my father but he did. He knew that it was my father's fault and not mine which put my mind at ease. When my father went to court over that, I do not think that they could have checked his record. He only got charged with drinking and driving and got off with the rest, which I could never understand.

My father continued drinking and ended up kicking my mother out of the house over and over but he always would find a way to get her back. Anyway, she would end up at my house which was only a few doors down. By this time, I was living with Daniel and we got along just fine. My father would always cause trouble and the neighbors would always find out what was going on. We could see into each other's house by the back sliding doors. One time when my father kicked my mom out and she came to our house. My dog Champ had arthritis really bad, and he was put on horse pills to help him. He was older by this time, the pills they had put him on caused his stomach to bleed a lot. There was blood everywhere. The doctors said that he had to be put to sleep. We were very upset but he was only suffering so we had to do it.

My mother was still living with us and a few weeks later, my father went out and bought a sheltie collie instead of a big one. Anyway, my mother and I would go to my father's house after he left for work in the morning and after work at night to see the new puppy. It was winter and we had a lot of snow but when my father got home from work, he would let the puppy out to play in the snow. Well, when he let the dog out it would run straight for our house and we would let him in to play with us. My father knew that he was at our house but that was the whole idea to get back in our good books again. When that did not work, he waited a few days and then he went out and bought my mother a new car that was really nice. It was fully loaded of course, as they always were and he knew that I was nervous driving my car as it was awful in the snow. He wrote a letter, put the keys in an envelope and put it in my mailbox. In the letter, he wrote about how much we would like the car and that it was good in the snow. We took the keys and drove it to work as my mother had worked at the same place as I did when the company she used to work for closed down. So we drove together every day and I always drove, as I loved to drive. That is the kind of person my father was he always was very giving and he would do anything for anyone when he wanted something. After a few weeks, my mother finally went home again.

I trained the puppy as I was very good at that and I owned this Himalayan cat and she was so pretty. She just loved the dog and when we went to the trailer, we always took both of them with us. If we went to visit our family, the dog would always sit in the driver's seat and the cat sat in the passenger's seat. It was so funny because one day we heard the car beeping and when we went out to look the dog was literally beeping the horn. It was as if he was saying "Come on let's go!" And every time after that the dog would always do this and the cat would always be sitting in the passenger's seat. The two of them got along so well that when I bred her, after she had the kittens I went to my parent's house to get the dog as I often did the cat took the dog up to see her new babies.

After a while, problems came and went. This one time changed our life for the worse. My father had been charged with molesting thirty- five children in our townhouse complex. All the neighbors were very upset and they got together and took a vote and kicked my father out of the townhouse complex, not that we blamed them. I was so ashamed and embarrassed and we had ten days to move out. When my brothers came to help us pack they found a hole in the wall and we thought my father had quit drinking after his impaired charge. My brother found over sixty bottles of empty vodka bottles in the wall. He was so sneaky all the time and we couldn't even tell whether he was drunk or not.

By this time both of my brothers had been married and had moved about twenty minutes away from us and it was actually right close to where my mother and I worked. This time my mother and father had moved in with my brother Danny until after my father's trial. When my father went to court he had to pay over ten thousand dollars for a lawyer and he had to go in front of the court of appeals. There were seven judges there. They finally put my father in jail for four months and after that, he was sent to a mental institute for another four months. Unbelievably, he just loved being in jail as long as no one knew what he was in there for and of course, no one ever did. My mother and I would visit him, as I did not want my mother to go alone. He was so happy to be in there, he would tell us all kinds of stories. I knew that he always wanted to be punished for what he did but I did not think that what he got was ever enough.

The big bosses where he worked for over twenty-six years went to see him in jail and of course they had to fire him but they paid him so much money that I could not even imagine. My father got enough to buy a new house and pay cash for it along with a new company car and a monthly pension. Now, he had lots of money, a brand new house and car. Crazy isn't it? After he did three months in jail, he got out early for good behavior then he had to go to the mental institute.

When he went to the institute, he talked to the top psychiatrist in Canada and he did con him somewhat but that's when they found out that there was something wrong with his brain. They also said that he did want to be punished for what he did but he could not stop himself. My father had told the doctor that the reason he went after children was because they were innocent and also the fact that he could control them as he could not control women. That made sense to them and he said that all of us had to have hated him for what he had done and that he did not blame any of us for that. He himself hated what he was doing and he wished that he could stop what he was doing to these helpless children but he did know that he needed help in order to stop himself. The psychiatrist put him on pills and one of the pills was to stop him from drinking because they said that the thought of molesting was always on his mind, but when he drank it would give him the nerve to carry out his thoughts and that is when he would molest children. When my mother and I went to see him I wasn't allowed to go in as he had been charged with molesting me when I was nine so I always had to wait in the waiting room. Even though I was twenty-four and had recently gotten married by this time I still was not allowed in to see him. They also told him that he only got the dog to get my mother to go home so he had to get rid of him. I had my own house by then so of course I took him in. After my father had spent three months in there, they began to let him in the waiting room for short periods of time to see me and trust me, it was a very small and very secure room.

After my father got out of the mental institute, he had quit drinking and so had my husband as he also drank a lot but was never ever violent. I also hated when he drank, as he also was an alcoholic. My father got a new job and was doing well but his heart was in very bad shape and after a while, he got a painful disease in his back and legs, which eventually left him disabled. The company that my husband worked at had laid many people off and he was one of them. By this time, the company that I had worked was also laying off people and my mother was one of them. I had been with them for ten and a half years and they laid-off everyone except ten people. I was one of the ten people that got to keep their jobs and I could afford to pay all of our bills but I was six months pregnant. My husband and I along with my parents decided to sell our houses and move to the country where my other family members lived.

I did not want to bring my daughter up in the city anyway so it worked out perfect. I also received a lot of money when I left the company that I worked for and with the money that we made on the sale of our house, we ended up with a nice profit, as did my parents. My father was already on a pension so we all were doing very well. We did move to where the rest of our family was and we decided to buy a house together with my parents. We finally found a nice house not far from town and the hospital because of my father's heart and we had a nice chunk of land. We had gotten the baby's room set up for my husbands and my baby to arrive. We should have known that this was just a fairy tale as the happiness had of course turned into problems. My father had started a big fight with us and even had tried to kick me in the stomach two days before I was supposed to have my baby. I had known as soon as I found out that I was pregnant that I could not have her naturally. My husband and I had no place to go at that time so we had no choice but to stay there. We told my father that we were either going to sell the house or he would have to buy us out and that is what he did. So then, we looked for somewhere else to live. Within a week we found a new place and we were allowed to move in right away, as it was already empty. It was far enough away from my father, he did not know where we had moved to and that was the way we wanted to keep it. After about a month my mother had left my father for good this time and moved in with us. That was when she finally filed for divorce.

The things that I saw sometimes were so scary that I never knew what to think. I saw a lot of dead people and even my grandmother, who had died when I was nine years old. It got to the point that I was frightened but I enjoyed the excitement all at the same time. I began believing in E.S.P, along with witchcraft and the devil. I always wanted to have séances and as I was sure that my father was the devil, I thought this was just in my blood. I was put on this earth to become a devil worshipper. I felt dark and empty inside anyway, so why not practice it? Maybe if I spent enough time trying spells and practicing séances, I just might find a way to be stronger than my father. I knew that I could not actually beat the devil. But when his back was turned and if he was not expecting it, maybe I could make him go away.

This does sound a little crazy to me now but back then, it made perfect sense to me. I began reading as much as I could on these subjects to make myself stronger and the more that I read it the darker it made me feel. I felt darker then I had ever felt before. I somehow began talking some of my friends into doing séances. We tried to get people that believed in ghosts to do them with us. It is really amazing to know the number of people who think they see ghosts or want to know things like if their house was haunted or not. I still can feel presences in houses if I want to put my mind to it. I think it is fun and exciting to know these things. I still can look at people and tell them things that they already know but do not understand. How I could possibly know what they knew when no one could have told me?

I still practice different things as I do believe in sight but it is different. Years ago, I was dark as was everything around me. I wanted to put a spell on him that would have killed him but I did not want to end up in jail. My mother always told my brothers and me that he was not worth spending our lives in jail over. She always said that what goes around comes around. I did have a hard time believing that one, as it seemed the only thing that had happened to me was bad. I had never imagined that my life was ever going to get better as it always seemed to just get worse. I was still young at that time in my life so all there was in my heart was hatred.

I may have spent a lot of time joking around with other people but that was just to cover up my true feelings. No one could truly ever know me. During the day around my friends, I was one person and at night, I was another. Everyone thought I was so happy at school that I knew I could cover up anything. I was also at the age where all the kids liked scary movies and stories that my devil worshipping just seemed okay with my friends. I never thought that there was anything wrong with worshipping the devil. I figured I had already been living with him anyway.

As time went by, I began spending more and more time reading spell books. I tried to figure out a way to put a spell on my father that would actually kill him without anyone finding out how he died. The only problem was, was that I could not tell whether my father was as gifted as I was and I wondered if he knew exactly what I was thinking. I often thought that if I had tried to hurt him that he might kill me instead. That made me too frightened to actually do anything that might harm him. I did want him gone for good but was not totally sure if anything like that would work on him. So I just read what I could find, thinking that one day I might just benefit from what I read. One night I went with my friend to her Aunt Jean's house because she thought that her house was haunted. When we got there, there was my friend Carla, her Aunt Jean, one of her aunt's friends Diana, Donna, Justine along with myself for a total of five people. Her aunt's friend had a big smoky quartz crystal ball with her and she told us that she could see things in this ball. I was quite interested in this, as I had read a lot about crystal balls. I asked her if she would mind very much if I tried to look at her ball and she said not at all. I had read that you were supposed to rub the ball to put your own energy on it so that you could empower it with your true reading so I proceeded to do so. As I did this I asked to see what was around me and what was I? I also had read that you were not supposed to look at the crystal inside the ball but actually focus on the power that you put into the ball. After a while it was supposed fog up around it and then you could see what you were supposed to.

As I did this I began to see myself with wolves around me and then we all began to run together as if I was part of their pack. I also saw myself in a past life and I was a witch that lived in this cabin in the woods along with my sister. It was like no one else could see us and we were adding ingredients to our boiling cauldron which was on a steel pole and there was a fire made of rocks on the outside and on the bottom of it. There were shelves all over the room. The shelves had jars with the weirdest things in them. This made me a little worried but the truth is that I always had a feeling that I really was a witch in more than one of my past lives. It seemed like time had went back even further and I saw this man place me on a table and there was a pentagram in the middle of this big room.

I lay on this table and it seemed like he had performed some type of spell on me with five other women. The women were going over my naked body back and forth, as he did this spell. When the spell was over with, I was put on this chair where I spent the rest of my life it seemed like. The only problem was, was that I could not move or talk ever again. I could however see everything and it was as if I knew everything there was to know about life and also about life after death. As I sat there in amazement, I saw a lot of dark grey clouds and at the end of them was a light that opened up and I saw many spirits inside this light. I have to admit that at the time, I did not know what to think and I stopped looking at the crystal ball but I knew that one day I myself had to own one of these balls.

After that, we all sat in a circle and talked about what Carla's Aunt Jean, wanted to find out during the séance. She began to tell us about her parents and how they were both dead and that a lot of strange things were occurring in her house all of the time. She told us that her family would be asleep at night and they would be awakened by the sound of something crashing down the stairs. When they went to investigate, they would find plates or glasses broken at the bottom of the stairs. They could not understand what was happening but she believed that her parents were mad at her as they did used to fight a lot when they were alive. She thought that they were also mad at her as she had gotten most of their furniture after they had died. As we began to get started, we had asked her what it was that she wanted to know. She had told us that she wanted to know if her parents were mad at her. She also wanted to know what had happened to her mother's gold watch as she was supposed to get it and save it for her own daughter when she was older. She told us that she searched everywhere for this watch and was unable to find it.

When we began the séance we all sat in a circle with a candle in the middle and we all concentrated on her parents even though we had no idea of what they looked like. The room was dark except for the candle in the middle of the circle and we began to see shadows around the room. Then all of a sudden, the radio started to play. We all jumped and one of us turned on the lights. That's when we noticed that the radio was not even plugged into the socket. We could not get it to stop for a long time and that freaked everyone out so we took a break until it finally stopped after about a half of an hour. We just sat there stunned for a while before we continued. After we had begun, again I had noticed that one of my friends looked like an old woman. At the same time another one of my friends had begun to cry saying that she had severe pain in her legs so we took a break again and it took quite some time before the pain had left my friend's legs.

None of us even knew what her parents had died from but we would soon to find out. Apparently, her mother was in a wheel chair with a very serious case of arthritis. When I had told her that I saw this older woman's face on my friend she was very surprised and ran to get her photo albums. As I looked through them I had no idea that this woman that I saw might have been her mother but when I finally found a picture of the lady I saw I pointed it out to her and it was in fact Jean's mother. We had taken another break and I went to the washroom. I had been to the washroom once before when I first got to her house. This time I had noticed this gold watch sitting on the back of the toilet. After I washed my hands I picked up the watch and brought it to Jean. She was so stunned that her eyes rolled back and she passed out. We ran for a cold cloth and when she had finally came to, she started to cry and proceeded to tell us that this was in fact her mother's watch. After her mother had died five years before this she could not believe that it just appeared out of nowhere and she was so happy that she finally had the watch that she searched for all of those years.

The night seemed to last forever and so many things happened that night that I will never forget it. When it was five thirty in the morning, we decided that it was time for bed. We all slept in the same room and we brought mattresses in from the other bedroom so that some of us did not have to sleep on the hard floor. We all thought that, this would be the end of all the things that were going to happen that night but much to our surprise, we were all wrong. As we laid there for a while we talked about what had happened that night. We were in Jean's master bedroom and we finally began to settle down to sleep. We turned the lights out and shut the bedroom door. We left the hall light on outside of the door on in case one of us needed to go to the washroom after we fell asleep. We were still awake when the bedroom door opened and then the long dresser drawer opened. We all sat up and then the dresser drawer shut and then the bedroom door. Well that shocked us and we all jumped up out of bed, took off out of that room, and ran down the stairs. Needless to say, we could not believe what happened until Jean told us that it was her parent's bedroom set and that her father kept his bills in that drawer with a lock on it so that no one could get into it and then it made sense to all of us. This had turned out to be quite a night and none of us got any sleep until we left in the morning and went home. I will never forget that night as long as I live.

After that, I began to play around with the Ouija board and I can honestly say that a friend and I actually became addicted to it. The spirits that we talked to seemed to be nice but every now and then, we got some mean spirits. My one friend became so afraid of it that she actually broke it in half and burnt it. Then it seemed as if the spirit stayed in the house so she had a priest come to the house and bless it. The truth is that every time I went over there I really had a feeling that there really was a bad spirit in her house. I could feel it. Whenever I walked down to the basement, I got a very weird feeling inside me that there was a bad presence very close to me. I know for a fact that on many occasions, I could feel spirits walk right through me and a lot of them were not the nicest spirits anyone would want to meet.

Many of the spirits that I have personally come in contact with seem to tell me all about themselves. For instance, I remember being able to tell exactly what they were like when they were alive. I have felt them, then I knew whether they were nice or not. On one occasion, I felt a spirit that was very mean and it was as if I knew his personality and what he looked like. I described him to my boyfriend, as I had a feeling that he knew this person in real life when he was alive. As it turned out, the man I had described to my boyfriend was his stepfather. I knew the man hated my boyfriend and was a very mean man that drank a lot. He was tall and skinny with a very bad temper and he died of cirrhosis of the liver. I had never seen a picture of him ever and I never knew anything about him at all until that day.

However, I was right about everything that I saw. I have to admit that my boyfriend could not believe what I had said because this man died long before I had come along but he truly did believe me. After that, whenever I told him anything like that, he did believe me. I remember that I had a feeling that his mother was very sick and was going to die soon and even though I did not want to upset him, I felt like I should tell him so that it would not be such a shock to him when the time came. For three months before she died I kept on telling him that he should be prepared ahead of time. I was not quite sure what he thought about what I was telling him but I just had to tell him, it would have bothered me to much if she died and he was so shocked that he might have had a lot harder time then he would have by being told him beforehand. Well, two days before she died I told him that she was going to die any time now, and she did die two days after I had told him that. He took the news much better than I thought he would have and I truly believe that I did help him by preparing him ahead of time.

Over the years, of all the spirits I have encountered, seemed like their life passed through me and I know so many things about them. I do believe this is true, as I have asked many different people if certain spirits looked a certain way or acted in ways that I could not possibly have ever known. Some people may think that it is impossible but it is not, as spirits are around us all the time. The only difference is some people refuse to believe so they overlook what is right in front of them. Every person in this world really does have a spirit guide. These guides help people in so many ways but most people just will not except that fact and they think people who believe in this sort of thing are crazy or just imagine it, but we are not imagining anything.

If people believe in God they should also believe in spirits, as God is a spirit, also. That I did not find out until I was a lot older. Bad spirits are people that die and are not happy in life so they are not happy in death either. I know that one bad spirit I saw was not at rest until his wife-died years later. Then she took him to heaven with her where they are now at peace.

I truly believe that people that live a hateful life turn away from the light, which is there to guide us to the most wonderful place anyone would ever want to be taken to. I know the difference now and for that, I am thankful, as I did live in hate for many, many years. The bad spirits seem to be in turmoil and it just seems to build in their souls as time goes by. This life is all there is until we die so if you do not make the best of it now you to may die in anger and your spirit may never find peace. Even though I did have a bad childhood, it was an experience that I was supposed to have in order to see things and feel the way I do today.

After we die and go to heaven we have to have learned whatever lessons in that life time that we were supposed to learn. Everyone has lived different life times as there is so many lessons to learn in each life. Before we even come back to earth we write our chart, which tells us what lessons we are supposed to learn before we come back to earth. The only problem is, is that when we return to earth we have no idea what we are supposed to learn so we spend our life learning different things. By the time we finally have learned everything that we should have, we die and go back to heaven and this cycle just continues until we have finally understood everything that we are supposed to know. When we are on our last life on earth, we become closer to the light and we also become more psychic. That is when we begin to understand the greater meaning of life.

Spirits are always around us even if we cannot see them. I do not believe in coincidences because if we pay attention there is a reason for everything that happens. So many things happen to everyone and they just do not realize that there is actually spirits around us all the time. For instance if your lights flicker for no reason, the chances are is that it is more than likely a spirit but we choose to ignore what is in front of us. So please pay more attention to the things around you and you will likely see what I mean, and there is nothing to be afraid of, as they will not hurt you in any way. The main reason that people choose not to see is really only fear of the unknown. So try to get over the fear and life will honestly be a lot more peaceful and loving than you could ever imagine.

I truly believe that the people in this world, who only think of themselves and never of others, are very selfish. To want to be the one taking but never giving, one will end up living a very sad and bitter life, as all the people around you see what you really are. I personally do not wish to be thought of after my death as a selfish and bitter person. I do know some people that are like that and all that anyone ever says about them is how greedy and sickening they are, which I do have to agree with. Some people only want good things to happen to them but I believe that one day they will be the ones in need and there will not be anyone there for them as a payback for the way they have always treated everyone else.

I never thought that the people who act and live this way every day would ever end up in a position where they would need help. Now, after seeing it happen to some of these people, I can say it is true; it does come back on them. On some occasions, I have seen people that are greedy and take everything from anyone that they can end up living their lives being alone.

Everyone they talk to turns around and do nothing but talk about them behind their back. As for me, I do not mind telling people what I see as I will tell them to their face, instead of behind their back. Even the people that I do tell what I think always turn it around, as if someone else made them do it. Now that is a joke to me as everyone does know himself or herself just as I do. However, people who make excuses for their own actions I believe will eventually get it back in one way or another.

As I always thought I must be evil because of my past, I now realize that everything in our life happens for a reason. I have told some people what I think of them but they have also told me what they think of me. I know who I am so why get mad? The ones who will not accept the truth make me laugh and feel very sorry for them. If you do not know who you are then how can you change your bad points? It's the people that think they are perfect are the ones that cannot be helped.

One day I decided to write a list of my good points and my bad ones. I was surprised to see how much hatred I have inside of me still after all that had happened to me. I admit that it is hard to get rid of hate but it could be done with time and help.

It has taken me well over thirty years to understand and learn how to heal myself. I have been depressed for years before I gained strength and courage to carry on with my life and finally learn the meaning of survival. If you are one of the people that can honestly say that you have survived a traumatic experience and have let go of all your anger and fear, then you should be very proud of yourself. Whether this has been physical, mental, sexual abuse, or any other traumatic experience, if you feel at peace with yourself and your life then you are a survivor and do not ever forget that. Never feel bad if sometimes you feel anger due to either seeing something on the television set or if something reminds you of something that has happened to you in the past as this will pass in time. I think this happens to everyone at one time or another. Just remember to stand your ground try to think of the better things in your life that make you happy and fight to survive. Remember that once you have survived the worst thing that has happened to you than you can survive anything that comes your way if you truly want to.

5

Darkness into the Light

After the death of my father, I thought that I would finally be free of all the bad thoughts that I had always felt about him. As it turned out, he and my mother had divorced one year earlier and he had gone from riches to rags. I could not believe that he turned out to be an unhappy person as I thought that he would finally be happy to get rid of all of us. It seemed so hard to believe that the man that threw us out of the house over and over and continually made us all believe that he hated us just was not true at all.

After my parents divorced, he was so lonely that he ended up marrying a woman that treated him just as bad if not worse, than what he did us. She beat him and hit him with his car and they fought a lot. As it turned out, he became petrified of her. They split up and she still would not leave him alone. He called the police on her time after time and they never did anything to help him. He got a dog, thinking the dog would bite her, but instead he had to give the dog back as it went after him instead.

Therefore, as it turned out, he lost everything and finally got his other wife to stay away from him. After they met, they were only together for five months before they got married. It only took three weeks of marriage before they had separated. My father ended up as a frightened man, as she kept on stalking him. The night that he had died, my cousin and his girlfriend, who had moved in with my father to keep him company, said that the woman my father was married to went to my father's house. They said that she had gone up stairs then came back down about twenty minutes later and then left the house. That was the last time anyone saw him alive. The next day my father was pronounced dead. This woman was not divorced from my father but he had a form from the lawyers that he was going to fill out to file for legal separation but he never had the chance.

The same night that he was pronounced dead, my cousin and his girlfriend went to go back to the house as they were living there. They told me that they had seen this same woman in the house around midnight looking all over the place. They saw her in the dark with a flashlight and they said that she was looking for something. Apparently, she had lifted all of the pillows on the couch and looked under the couch. She then searched the closets, kitchen cupboards and drawers. According to my cousin, she had not found whatever it was she had been looking for because she stormed out of the house. After she had left, they went into the house and they began searching all over the place to see if they could find whatever it was that she had been looking for. As it turned out, they found a letter that my father had wrote stating that he feared for his life. He believed that she was going to kill him. There was also a list of things that he had about how she was beating him up. They also found pictures my father had taken of her and her father taking things out of my father's house that did not belong to her. My cousin was very worried that she had smothered my father in his sleep the night before. They brought the letter and pictures to our attention, then my mother and my father's sister went to the police with them. The police sadly enough, ignored everything. This woman was very frightening, even looking at her was scary, never mind trying getting into an argument with her. I personally think that her parents who had a lot of money might have given the police a very hard time if they had pursued the matter at hand.

The whole family wanted an autopsy done on my father to find out just how he died. Since my father was not divorced yet, she would not allow it. Then she tried to fight my mother for the life insurance policy which my father had left to my mother, but she never did win that one, I am happy to say.

Therefore, my father's death is still a mystery to all of us. No one knows the truth as the police never did help us. It is not very good to count on the police sometimes. They do not always try to help as everyone might think. From the time I was a child until the day my father died. They never helped us at all, I am very sorry to say. My mother called me the day of my father's death. She was living in the same town as he did. My husband, my daughter and I had just moved back to the city a few months earlier. My husband went back to work at a previous job he had. At any rate, my mother was at my father's house when the coroner pronounced him dead. She told me that his diamond ring was taken, along with his expensive watch they were supposed to go to my two older brothers. The day before his death, he had told his sister that he had a lot of money on him and was going to go Christmas shopping for all of us. But as it turned out not only did he end up dying, but all his money from his wallet had conveniently disappeared. She stayed there until they took him out of the house. My mother was living with my father's father and sister at that time so they were there with her also.

I had a hard time believing that it was true but my mother confirmed it. She phoned me and we talked for about an hour or so. I thought at first that I was finally free of him, but I just felt numb. I really could not describe the feeling but something just did not feel right. The funny thing was that even though my father had molested me for all that time, when he was sober he was a very nice person. As my mother and I talked, we reminisced about some of the things that my father had done in the past that were really funny. He did have a great sense of humor despite all of his faults. We laughed about many of the bad things he did, as well as the good ones. I felt as if he was listening to us and laughing along with us. This may sound a little strange to you but over the years, even some of the bad became funny because of the fact that he sometimes in anger, would end up funny by either falling or saying the wrong thing.

One time my brother went upstairs to phone the police to come over. When he came down the stairs to tell my father, my father said that he was going to call the police, also. The funny part was that when my father was calling the police he held the receiver down and he acted as if he was talking to them and all of a sudden, the phone rang. It was the police calling back to see if we still wanted them to come or not. Well, the look on my father's face was just priceless. We laughed about things like that to this day. That night that he died, I truly felt like my father was laughing right along with us the whole time. That would have made perfect sense to us, because that was the way he was. He always did like a good joke.

I did not really want to go to the funeral but I decided I had to see for myself if his death was real and if my nightmare was finally over. We all were there on our side of the family but the woman that he had recently married had to cause trouble. That is what she seemed to do best from what my father's letter had stated. So her and her parents were the only other people there and they sat alone on one side of the funeral home and our family and friends sat on our side of the funeral home as no one wanted to be anywhere near his wife's side of the family. There were even people standing in the back. I would have to say that we did have a lovely service and that for some reason my mother had to pay for it as his new wife refused to have anything to do with anything that cost money. She even got a lawyer to try to fight for the life insurance policy that my father had left in my mother's name, as he really did love her. The fact that they had been together for thirty-two years must have meant something to him. After my parents had split up, he had told his sister that he was not going to change that as he figured we had suffered enough because of him. He would not change it.

Well, after the funeral was over, I believed that he was really gone now and this would be the end of my worries or so I thought. After that, I stayed for about a week or so before I returned to the city. During this time, I could not get him out of my mind at all. It was like a big nightmare starting all over again. I felt like he was trying to tell me something as I felt like his presence was always around me.

All the years that I had spent seeing, let's say ghosts and spirits none had frightened me anywhere near as much as he did. I had seen ghosts ever since I was the age of five. Seeing ghosts, even the bad spirits might have frightened me when I was young, but this was the most frightening thing of all. At first I thought to myself that I was just imagining things, but I knew deep down that there was no way possible that I could have been. The first thing that I thought was that he was trying to tell me was something about his death. I thought that we were missing some piece of information that he needed for me to see. However I still, to this day, think that someone did something to him and one of the first clues was the fact that my mother found a bottle of vodka in the garbage. Now, we all knew for a fact that my father would have died before he would have ever thrown booze in the garbage and I would bet that any true alcoholic would agree to that. My father had never ever thrown any type of alcohol in the garbage or down the sink. I do believe this is the total truth no matter what anyone might have ever said.

I became so afraid to be alone. I had a hard time sleeping, as he just would not go away. If I was driving, I would see him in the back seat of my car or in the middle of the road. I was getting more and more spooked every day. Getting him to leave me alone seemed impossible.

I could not do anything without him being there. I was afraid to take a shower or even look in the mirror as I could always see his eyes in my own. I could also always see or feel his presence beside me. I was afraid to go to sleep, even if my husband was in the bed with me. I was sure that after a few months of him being everywhere that this was never going to end. I knew that he was not hurting me, but I was too frightened to figure out what he wanted me to do. It got to the point that I thought I was cracking up due to the fact that he would not leave me alone. I thought that after about four months of watching my husband get drunk that it might have something to do with it. I could not stay with him anymore as his drinking at that time seemed to be more important than his daughter or myself. I felt like there was no escaping it. I had begged my husband time and time again to please quit drinking. But he would not listen to me at all. I finally had enough and went to live with my brother for about four or five months. I got along very well with my brother and his wife and his three children.

We had a lot of fun living there but we really did not have enough room for my daughter and myself. We had to sleep on the floor in the dining room. However, they took us in and for that, I was very grateful. My brother's wife and I would walk a long way with four children to go shopping and out for lunch. We would have four children and a stroller for the younger ones and a buggy full of groceries and we would walk there and back again in the middle of winter. We did have fun and it would tire out the children so that when we got home they would get tired from the nice cold air and be ready for their afternoon nap. We did look forward to that after that long walk. Then my brother's wife and I would get to have a tea and watch our favorite soap story on the television set until they would wake up. Our children got along very well. They were all close in age so they never fought that much at all. My brother did a paper route every morning before work and on Saturday nights, I would go help him as the Sunday morning paper was very large and we would have to put it all together. We would have to get up at one thirty in the morning on Sunday morning to get the papers delivered on time. We had a lot of fun, as we would meet up with his wife's brother and cousin as they also delivered the paper. I got along very well with my brothers wife's brother as we used to work together for years at the same company. I have to admit that we all had a lot of fun doing that but I knew that I would have to move out soon enough.

I also felt like I needed to be with my mother. One day I left the country. When I moved back to the country, my daughter and I also moved in with my father's father and sister along with my cousin and my mother who lived there also. I tried to think that now I would be safe but he was still there. While all this was going on I remember how frightened I really was all of the time and I did not know what to do. My daughter and I slept together in the back bedroom and I had many sleepless nights, as I knew that my father was watching me.

Finally, I decided to tell the rest of the family what was happening. My aunt told me where to go to get some professional help. I have to admit that this did seem a little hard to do as trying to tell a stranger that my dead father would not leave me alone was very hard to talk about. However, I knew I needed the help as nothing else that I had tried had worked up until this point.

It took me a while but I did finally get up enough strength to call for help. I needed therapy more than I had thought at the time. I told her that my father molested me and that he had died recently and I even told her about him not leaving me alone even in death. She gave me different books to read about in order to help me heal myself and to take away the fear along with different assignments to do. I put a lot of effort into trying to heal myself but it was hard as my father still would not leave me alone. I tried everything and I have to admit that I did begin to feel a bit better about myself but my father was still around me all the time.

After a long while of therapy, he still would not leave me alone. I would be driving down the road and I would see him standing there. You know that even though he was a ghost, I could not bring myself to hit him with the car. I usually would swerve out of the way in order to miss him. Even knowing that, I could not do anything to him. I still could not hurt him. I recall how he would be touching my back or shoulder while I did the dishes or how sometimes I would see him in the back seat of the car when I was driving. I even had to sit in the corner of any room in the house just so that he wouldn't be behind me as I thought that if he was around me I had to be able to see him and know what he was doing at all times. I think the only thing that went through my mind at that time was that he was trying to either kill me or send me to the funny farm. After spending a long time in therapy, I finally gave up as I believed that nothing was ever going to get my father to leave me alone.

In July of 1995, after being hurt at work in January 1993,

I was going for physiotherapy due to the severe pain I was having as a result of the accident. I had been working for some time then and I liked my job. On the day of my accident, I was coming back from break which was upstairs, and as I got to the big heavy wooden swinging doors I was accidentally hit by a very nice person who had to run with a cart of bananas. The big wooden doors had been very hard to go through with a cart of anything. We were both short and the holes that were drilled in the doors at the time were too high for either of us to see out of. Anyway, as I had just got to the doors, I had tried to push it open but he had entered the doors at the same time as I did and that's when I was hit. When you were bringing a cart of anything through the doors, you had to run and push both doors at the same time as the cart was not small enough to just go through one door. Well, we hit at the same time. I smashed my face on the door and that snapped my neck back and then I flew backwards about ten feet and landed on my lower back. I thought that my head was going to explode and I felt that way for over eight months or more.

I still have migraines and I will wake up with a migraine in the morning and it will last all day and most of the time it will last even longer than that. If I wake up in the morning and the sun is shining in my face then that is all it takes for me to end up with a migraine in the morning. I have a very hard time sleeping for any length of time do to the pain that I suffer. I am lucky to get three to four hours sleep all night that is actually on a good day and that does not help the pain at all. My neck, shoulders, arms, wrists, hands, hips, legs, and even ankles and feet still bother me quite severely every single day as this has given me Fibromyalgia, which is a very painful disease. To this day if I don't take my headache pills and a lot of pain pills for everything that is wrong with me, which is more pills than I care to count, I start having breathing problems. I take a breathing pill and four puffers to help me breath and a machine that I put two different kinds of medicine in and I cannot go without them or I will suffer for the whole day. Not that I do not already suffer terrible on a regular basis, but it would be really worse if I don't. As the years had passed, I have gotten a lot worse than I was. This in turn caused me to have other illnesses like a very serious lung disease called Chronic Obstructive Pulmonary Disease (C.O.P.D.), diabetes and gastritis. I also have a hard time with degenerating arthritis and osteoporosis. I have been this way for a long time and I need to walk with two canes or my walker. I am dealing with this every single day. I do believe for a fact that without my medication I would not be able to walk at all – which, I pray, will never happen. I have to admit that on many occasions I have fallen or pushed myself to hard and have had no choice but to crawl around on my hands and knees to get around because the pain is so severe that I just cannot walk at all. It has gotten to the point where I cannot even walk to my own mailbox that is at the end of my driveway.

I finally moved to the country where I still am to this day. The house I bought is now only one level but it used to have a sunken living room. I had to get someone to raise the floor due to the four stairs. Now that I suffer with severe pain every day, I cannot climb the stairs. When I first bought this house, my father was still following me around and I was still very frightened of him. I think back on how the pain was worse than he was, as he never hurt me physically after his death. I began ordering him around as he was even following me into the washroom. I had to put an end to that so I would yell at him and started to lay some rules down and I do believe that this may sound off the wall but it worked. He was never ever allowed in the bathroom with me and he even agreed to it.

I had not been to see my counselor in almost three years by this time. After seeing her for about a year and a half I did feel better about me emotionally but everything that she tried never did seem to make my father go away. I figured that there was nothing anyone could do to help me get rid of a ghost. At the time, I never ever believed in God, as I felt like I was always being punished for something ever since I was five years old. By this time in my life, after being hurt at work and trying to raise my child, along with dealing with the worse pain all over my body that I never could even begin to think anyone ever could live with. I struggled every day and still do. However, nothing ever worked to make my life easier. My daughter was young and there was always a lot of work to do just to make it through each day. I have to say that I truly believed that I was being punished for ninety percent of my life.

My father had already been dead for over four years by this time and he still would not leave me alone. It was as if he wanted to make me do something for him but I was too angry with him to care. I had a feeling that there was something I had to do in order to make him leave but he couldn't tell me and I knew deep down that I had to figure it out for myself but I really didn't know how. I have to say that I had enough problems of my own, never mind trying to help my father who had caused me so much pain in the past. I just wanted peace in my life for once and it seemed like I was never about to get any. I tried to just live my life as each day came and deal with what I could even though I knew that my father was always there. I wanted my father to leave me alone so I had to try other options to get him to leave. I tried to get my father's mother who had also died years before, to try to help me but she could not either. This was one thing that I had to do on my own. My grandmother had died when I was nine. I always saw her every now and then over the years but when I told my family I was never truly sure if they believed me until a week before my grandmother's daughter died. My aunt's son had also seen her for the first time and I think, it was also the last time that my cousin saw my grandmother. It was then that he knew that his mother was going to die, as she was very sick with cancer and had been in the hospital for a very long time.

From the day my father died, along with the pain and housework and making sure my daughter was being looked after, I became so worn out that I thought I just couldn't carry on anymore. Everything I did I suffered so bad that I would just collapse to the floor and would not be able to get up for a while until I got a bit of strength back. My life was becoming more and more difficult to take. Then, this one night I was just so worn out and so weak I did not think I could carry on anymore. I went to bed but I had always had a hard time sleeping due to the pain. I was still awake at the time but I really have to admit that I thought I was soon about to die as I felt so weak.

As I lay in bed, I felt as if I had been in the dryer for three days. My body felt like it was bruised from head to toe. As I lay in bed all that went through my mind was how I would carry on and continue to raise my daughter. It was a bad point in my life and all I seemed to do was cry. I had lost a lot of weight I was at ninety-four pounds, which made it even harder for me to fight on a day-to-day basis.

I still had no proof that God existed and all I felt was anger, anger towards what my father did and now with this disease. I just could not believe in anything. All that went through my mind was "Why did this happen to me?" I just could not believe that if there was a god. Why did he make my life so horrible? I had never really prayed for anything other than for loved ones who were dying but they died anyway, so I had no reason to believe anything that had to do with God. Being haunted by my father did not seem to help me either.

As I lay in bed one night crying, the only reason I wanted to stay on this earth for was my one and only daughter. She meant everything to me. As I said before, I did see ghosts on a regular basis and they always seemed to frighten me except for my grandmother. As l lay in bed, crying and worn out from the pain I could hear the voice of someone that I had never heard before. It was if I did not see anyone around, as I usually did, but the feeling of love was so strong that I could not even begin to describe it. I felt my soul begin to float upward towards a very bright light. I felt no pain, only love. It felt so amazing! It was like nothing I had ever felt before.

6

The Light Above

As I floated upwards, the feeling that was in my heart just kept getting stronger and stronger. Then this voice was talking to me. It was like there was no one there but I felt a very strong presence. I could not actually see anyone but I felt what this voice was saying. I ended up in this huge room with light all around me and it had a very large white table in it. I still did not see anyone but at the same time, I felt the presence in my heart. This voice told me that I was put on this earth for a very good reason, just like everyone else and that I still had a lot to learn. I know this may sound odd but this was my destiny that I had known before I was sent back to earth after my last death.

The funny thing was I already knew I had many past lives so this did not seem so odd to me at all. The voice explained to me that every being decides there own destiny before they are reincarnated back to earth. So I understood that everyone keeps coming back to earth as they have to have completed every lesson that there is in each of our lifetimes. When I asked what my lessons in this lifetime were, it was as if I had to figure it out for myself. I realized that the anger I had felt was meant to be and now I had to decide what I was going to do to change these feelings in order for me to lead a better life.

I asked for a tour while I was up there and was surprised that it was granted. The first thing I saw was these beautiful golden gates that were rounded at the top. I think they were a symbol as I have never seen them since. As we entered, I saw spirits everywhere and the love inside was unexplainable. I think that many of these spirits turn into guides and they are guides for everyone on earth. I gather that they remain guides forever and are never sent back to earth again. Then again, that is questionable as I think that, they have also completed all their lessons on earth and are now there to help us.

Even though most people cannot see them, they are there to help us in many ways such as if you were about to do something, then you get the feeling you should not, that is one of your guides, not just your intuition. As we continued our tour, I realized that in Heaven it is like one big family and everyone knows everything about everything. There are no questions to be asked. If you, for instance, want a beautiful garden or a house, you can just think it and there it is. When I was there that is what I wished for and it was there. In addition, I wished for a white walkway with a bridge and a waterfall and it was there, just like that. I was amazed at that and at how healthy looking everyone was.

I felt no pain or hate at all while I was there. Another thing that I noticed was that no one had beds as if no one slept, and everyone was always busy doing something. The most amazing thing of all was that Heaven was never ending; no matter where we were there was no end.

I was also told that while I was in the big white room with the large table that everyone writes their chart for their next life on earth before they even come back to earth again. You see that in every lifetime, there are certain lessons to be learned and once you learn them all for that lifetime, then you die. When you are in Heaven after that life is over, whatever it is that you have not learned, you keep coming back to earth until you have completed all there is to be learned. Then you finally have the honor of staying in Heaven forever. I also realized that when you are in Heaven that you learn different trades. For instance, some people are doctors and you study to make a cure for a disease. Well, when you return to earth, you might get side tracked for a while. But eventually you enter a field of work that will lead you to your true path in that life time. The chances are that you will likely never understand why this happens. But the truth is that you have already learned this in Heaven. It is always in your chart before you come back to earth. So here on earth you need to relearn the lessons on your chart. These lessons you already knew the answer to in Heaven even if it takes years to figure out. You will eventually figure it out no matter what you think. So never give up on what your heart tells you as it is always the right decision in the end.

Just the thought of being there was a very precious gift and I have to admit that I did not want to leave there at all. When our tour was over, I realized I had learned more than I had learned in my whole life on earth. As I floated back down and entered my body, again I have to say everything that I thought or felt changed for the best. I really wished that I could have stayed there but I wanted to be the one to raise and protect my daughter and not anyone else. I was really thankful for that experience.

I felt the pain all over again but my life was about to change. I had a really hard time getting to sleep that night but I would never have given up that experience for anything else, other than my daughter. When I finally fell asleep, it was like the first time I had slept peacefully in my life. For that, I am grateful. When I woke up the next morning, the pain was awful but I did something that I never thought I would ever even dream of doing before. As I got up and walked towards the kitchen I called to my father and after years and years of hate, I finally understood why he could not leave me alone after his death. I saw him right in front of me, I said, "Dad, I truly forgive you for what you did to me." and I realized that what he did to me was actually a gift. He never hated me; my father gave me the gift of sight. If it was not for what he had done to me, I would have never been able to leave my body for all these years. When he molested me the very first time, I then jumped out of my body and even though what he did was wrong it was meant to be whether I knew it or not. After I explained this to my father and forgave him, I finally set him free. I did watch him as he floated upward to Heaven and I have to say that was his best day ever.

I still am honored that I can now visit him whenever I want to and I am happy that I set him free. When I see him now I know that he is proud of me. Therefore, no matter what he did and how he made me feel, the gift of sight was a gift of love that he was meant to give to me.

I do not want people to think that being molested or raped is okay for people to do because it is wrong. These people should be punished for what they do because no one should have to be put through that. Our society does not seem to realize what the victims of abuse go through on a day-to-day basis. Well, I went through it and understand the necessity for more places for the victims to go to for help. I do believe that when someone is charged for abuse they seem to get some help, if the authorities feel it is necessary. Then there are some cases where the victims are blamed for causing sexual abuse due to what they were wearing or for teasing them. Well, there is still no excuse for this as no still means no. No person actually causes anyone to abuse another - this is their problem and no one else's. Abusers blame everyone except themselves. However, in truth, this is always their problem and no one else's.

My father was sent for therapy as he had a mental illness which was proved later on in life. That was still no excuse for what he did to a lot of children including myself. The problem remains that my father received help and not one single child ever did. To my years of knowledge on this issue, there must come a time where the victims come first. The courts should send the victims for help along with the abusers. I am positive that if the victims had more help there would be a lot less suicides or drug and alcohol problems in the world today. I am thankful that I got the help I needed, even if no one offered it to me as a child. I was twenty-nine years old when I finally realized I needed help in order to carry on with my life. If I never went for help, I just might have ended up dead by now. Now I am truly proud of myself for what I have accomplished over the years and I wish all victims could feel the way that I do. Ever since I had the pleasure of visiting Heaven, I cannot believe how much better I have become. I am not saying that you have to go to church, as I never have and still do not but I now know that there is life after death and it is more than I had ever thought possible. Once you can forgive the abusers and open your heart, you would be amazed at the love that you have missed out on due to living with hate, as I once did.

Freedom is like lifetimes of learning and going through everything from rich and poor, bad and good or the difference between love and hate. Once we have accomplished everything, I guess I do believe that some of us become spirit guides to help others on earth. Even though I still have a lot to learn, I know that this is my last time on earth. I will then become a spirit guide to help others in need as I feel that this is my calling.

When my father was haunting me, I now know that was his way of apologizing for what he had done but I was so afraid of him that I did not see it. Now that he is in Heaven, I am not afraid to visit him anymore. I not only visit him but I can see anyone that has died. Many people cannot see things but I have learned different ways. The main thing that frightens people is the unknown but if you can open your heart, I know that anyone can do it. We are put on earth to grow into a whole person and what I think happens is that we are reincarnated over and over again until we understand everything in this world along with the unknown and once we have learned everything then, and only then, are we all set free.

I had never meditated at all before but I always managed to see many things. It is a gift but anybody can learn how to see things that they never saw before. I always feel a bright light above me now, which I could never see before. I could leave my body ever since I was first molested which I think happens to a lot of people but it is scary at first. For me, this was always my escape as it is for many people, I am sure of that. I think about the first time it happened and the reason this did happen was that I was in shock. I needed a way to escape and my soul just jumped out of my body to protect me from fear of what was happening to me. Everyone has fear in their life, whether they believe it or not, but many people refuse to discuss it with anyone. If you face your fear, you would see that there is a whole other world out there. I find that men have a harder time expressing their feelings than females do but that is really just fear of what people might think and they are frightened of the unknown. My father was the type of person who would never say he was sorry for what he did but it came back on him even after death. I always wished that he would say he was sorry, as it made me resent him that much more because he made me think I was always the one who was to blame. It did come back on him, as he never had the chance to truly live a happy life. I was always cold towards him and always kept my distance as I thought he hated me for what he said was always my fault.

When I had my daughter, I finally broke all ties with him. Even though I knew it bothered him. I was not about to put my daughter through anything that I went through, so he never got to see his own granddaughter. I know this bothered him but if I didn't protect her, then who would? I am truly sorry for the fact that she never knew him but that was something I would never change if it meant that she would go through what I did. I am sorry that it did have to turn out that way.

DAD

Dad, the years I spent with only hurt and pain.
As the time went by, I thought pure love I could never gain.
You did always give me everything I could ever want,
Nevertheless, material things never did ever buy you my love.

You were so kind to everyone in every way,
As you always gave to anyone, each and every day.
You did sin, as all people do.
As for mistakes, we have all made quite a few.

Now I know this was to be my fate.
Your sense of humor brought many people joy.
As for us who lived with you, we only felt the pain,
This made us resent you, no matter what we gained.

We all fought between the love and the hate.
After years of this, I thought I would never recover.
Now that I have, I forgive you with an open heart.
So, I now thank you for this pure gift of sight.

Now I know when I die I will go to Heaven,
For now I have seen the extraordinary Heavenly bliss.
No one could ever ask for more than this.

7

The Spirit World

As I have stated before, I have been able to leave my body since I was molested for the first time when I was five. I also stated that I always knew what my body was doing along with my spirit. I now realize how psychics do this. If you are one of the people who can do this then you are way ahead of the game. I have seen many spirits over the years but you must try to stay calm, they cannot really hurt you. They usually only appear to get help or if it is someone you know, they might need forgiveness for something they might have done to you that keeps them from going to Heaven.

If you have seen spirits before, you might have tried to block them out as I have done in the past. I would have to say that I now wish I had never done that, they needed my help and I now feel as if I let them down. I want you to know that there are spirits and or angels around you all of the time. Many people are frightened of the unknown. I have met some spirits that have touched my shoulder or smacked me on the bum but I think that has happened to many people but they do ignore these things and some are to busy to even notice.

There is one thing that I have never known and that is how you tell whether the spirits that you see are all ready dead or if they jump out of their bodies as I do. That is one thing I have to find out. If spirits come to us for help then are they really dead or alive? This one night I recall very well, my daughter was asleep and I was still up at four o'clock in the morning. Anyway, there was this spirit of a young girl and she was twelve years old. She was at this beach with her family and she somehow got lost. She was at the water and when she got out I noticed that she had a blue one peace bathing suit on that had a white stripe going down one side to the other side. Anyway, when she was out of the water she started to look for her parents. The problem was that she began to walk in the wrong direction. The beach was packed full of people and she just got lost.

She ended up walking too far and it was getting late and she was getting cold. Where she ended up was way out of the way from people and a place that was full of rocks and patches of trees here and there. She was so afraid and she was cold so she sat down behind this big rock to block herself from the wind. She was crying when this older man came along. It was getting dark and he told her not to worry he would stay with her and in the morning, he would help her get home. This man was very tall and he was wearing a beige trench coat so he took it off and gave it to her to keep her warm. There was something about this man that she did not trust and it was not just because he was a stranger. I felt the same way when I first saw him but I was not sure if she was dead or not. Anyway, this bothered me so much because I had a feeling that he was going to kill her. I could see that he had an old cabin in the woods only about a mile from where they were. This bothered me so much that I had to call the police to tell them. At that time, I was sure that she was alive and I knew that her parents had a search party looking for her, but they were going the wrong way.

When I called the police, I thought that they might think I was crazy but they did not. I told them the whole story but I did not know the whole name of the beach, I only knew that it had the word "Edge" in it. I thought that was the first word but this could have been anywhere in the world for all I knew and I had only called one police station. After giving all the information to the police, I still could not get to sleep. I had noticed for a long time that my daughter was able to see things as I did. Mainly I noticed because of some of the things that she would say at one time or another. Anyway, I decided that I had to wake her up to prove to myself that this was true. As I woke her up, I asked her to concentrate and tell me if she saw anything about a young girl.

I have to tell you that I was surprised when she began talking about a twelve-year-old girl that got lost at the beach. She told me everything I had already told the police, including her hair color and the stripe on her blue bathing suit, right down to the man that gave her the trench coat. She knew everything that I did, including the older man's cabin that was about a mile through the woods. She even told me that the search party was going in the wrong direction. She also thought that she was still alive and that this man was going to kill her. I knew that she did not hear me on the phone so I told her that I called the police but they did not know anything. I asked her if she knew where this place was and she said that she could see the road but was not sure where it was exactly. She did seem to be good at directions while I am not, so she thought that we could find it if we went north. The only problem was that we did not know where to go.

By the next day, she had been killed and we both knew it. The police had thought that she had drowned by that time and were searching the water but I do not think they ever found her. However, we both knew that she was killed in the woods near the man's cabin. It turned out that we could not help her and we both felt bad knowing this. The problem is how you really know if this is past, present, or the future. I am still trying to figure this out and I wish I knew where I could find this out. For all I know, this girl might have already been dead and just could not rest in peace because of what she went through.

Another time my daughter came home from school and told me that, she heard this other girl screaming for help. She told me that another boy in her class had heard it, too, and they both looked at each other at the same time. Then she heard this girl say "Please, please, somebody help me!" and again the same boy looked at her and she looked at him at the same time. He did not say anything that day but the next day he went up to her when she was alone. He said, "You might think I am crazy but did you hear that girl screaming for help yesterday?" My daughter said "Yes!" But she did notice that it scared him so they agreed not to tell anyone else about it.

She asked me how to tell if this was just happening to this girl or did it already happen. I told her I did not know and said I have the same problem. Even though I can sometimes tell, that things have happened years ago but that is only because of the clothes they are wearing or if they tell me the year. I guess that I should ask these spirits right away instead of not knowing the truth.

When I was a lot younger, the spirits that I saw really frightened me as they were usually killed in brutal ways. I can recall seeing these people all in this attic. This evil man hanged them there. I could not believe that there was so many of them and some were children. They told me that they were in some type of cult and these people were sacrificed as part of a punishment or something. Now that scared me, but at the same time I knew that this happened, a couple of hundred years ago and they still were not at peace. At that time, I did not know how to help them go to the light. I know now that fear was my biggest problem.

As the years went by, I have to say that most of the spirits did in fact scare me but now I know why. One reason was because of the fact that I was already being molested on a regular basis, so I was always afraid to begin with. The other reason was that I did think that I was the devil's daughter because I believed that my father was the devil himself. It always seemed like the spirits that I saw were mean but I now think that they just needed help. Because of the way I felt, I think that I was living in the dark so I seemed to attract dark scary spirits.

I think that most children are so innocent that they do see other things because they do not have any reason to believe otherwise. I have noticed that many children that have imaginary friends act as if they are real. I would have to say that I do believe that they are in fact, seeing real spirits that are not imaginary at all.

My brother has three children. Well, one of them would wake up screaming at night saying that there was someone standing at the end of his bed. This happened for many nights and it was only a few months after my father had died. When they asked him what this person looked like my brother and his wife were surprised to hear that this man sounded a lot like my father. They had not seen my father for a couple of years and their son was quite young the last time he had seen him so he did not remember him. One night they decided to get out the photo album to see if their son would recognize anyone in it. Well, their son saw a picture of our father and he said that was the man that he was seeing. Therefore, their son slept with them for a while then they decided to put the two boys in the same room to make him feel better and my father did leave him alone after that.

When I was a child, I did not know who I was afraid of more, my father or the spirits. Mind you, I never had a sister to share a room with so I lived in fear. I did not want to sleep in my parent's bedroom as my father was real and I already knew what he could do to me. By the time, I was seven or eight I started asking to have a friend over or if I could spend the night at their house. I was lucky that they let me do that all the time, even on school nights.

Even when I got older, I always saw spirits all the time. I could walk into any house and know if there was a spirit there or not. Even though I was afraid of spirits, I was interested at the same time. I do believe that was why I began doing séances. I thought at the time, that they were all evil but they were really not. It was me that was really frightened so that made me think they were evil too. There was only one spirit at that time that I knew for sure was not frightening and that was my grandmother who had died when I was nine. She had multiple sclerosis and was in the hospital for over twenty-five years. We would go and get her on the weekends. All of us took turns and after she died, I thought she would come and see me because she was trying to protect me from harm.

I can recall that a few years ago I began to see this little boy all the time. It was in the house that I live in now. I really felt like I had known him in a past life. Well, the house that is beside mine was an old school house. They had left it there, back when schoolhouses were small and in the country. This school had been closed down for years as they built new and bigger ones since then. There was a friend of ours that used to live in my house. From the very first time I had come to visit him I felt like I was finally home. So I told him if he ever wanted to sell it, I wanted to buy it from him. Anyway, my wish finally came true. I always felt like I had been here before at the same time, I knew that I would never move no matter what. This was where I belonged and that was odd because I spent most of my life in the city, which was over two hundred miles from here.

I have been in this house since 1995 and I never plan to leave until I die. Well, this one year I kept hearing children running and playing outside on this property. This house is on the top of a hill now but years ago, this area was just a big empty field. They just brought lots of dirt in when they built this house. Every night I would see the shadow of a person running past the front of the house. On many occasions, I got my boy friend to go and check to see if someone was there. He always said that there were no footprints on the snow. He lived in town so my daughter and I would go to visit him in town a lot as she had many friends there.

For two to three months, I told my boyfriend that there was a young boy who kept trying to communicate with me. I have to say that I swore I knew him in a past life as I could remember sitting on the front step of the school and talking to him all the time. He was my best friend all through school. The problem was that I did not want to help him as I was going through a lot of pain at the time so I tried to block him out of my head.

I knew all about him and that he had been murdered for something that wasn't his fault. Years ago, he had a little brother who was too young to walk so his parents had him in one of those old-fashioned prams. Anyway, where they lived there was a big hill out the back of their house. This boy was outside with his parents and it was windy outside that day. The baby who was in the carriage, was on the edge of the hill. This hill was very steep and covered with trees all the way down. The parents just left the carriage there without even thinking. Well, a strong gust of wind came along and the carriage began to roll. The boy tried to chase after it but it was to late. The carriage and baby went down the hill and hit a tree. The carriage was destroyed and the baby died.

The mother knew that it was not the boy's fault but the father blamed him for killing his other son. The father was so mad that he paid this other man one thousand dollars to kill his other son. This man came over one day after school. He was big he had dark hair and a very long beard. The boy's parents were there that day too. They had lots of money and they were always well dressed. The mother was very nice and had no idea of what was about to happen. The boy's parents were standing there talking to the teacher. The man who was paid to kill the boy had a knife and he began running after the boy. The boy got to the back of where my house is now and tripped over a rock that was lying in the middle of the field. The teacher looked and started to chase after the man to stop him but it was too late. The man stabbed the boy in the back and the boy died. That man died a few months later of a heart attack. The teacher was so upset that he felt the guilt until his death.

After that, he and the boy hung around this house. When the boy could not get help from me, I thought that he decided to leave me alone but I was wrong. I had only told my boyfriend what had happened and I told him everything from what they looked like to what they wore. I told him not to tell anyone including my daughter, as I did not want to scare her. He said that he would not so I just tried to forget all about it.

My daughter's bedroom was facing the front window where I had seen this boy running by all the time. Her bedroom was right beside the living room. Well, I did quit seeing this boy but I had no idea that something else was going on. My daughter began to try to sleep with me every night for a long time. I never could understand why, as she had not tried that for quite a few years. I tried to tell her that she was getting too old to be sleeping with me but she kept on asking every night.

Then one night I told her that it was time to sleep in her own room and she began to cry. This was odd I thought, so I asked her what was wrong. She said that she was going crazy and I said "What do you mean by that?" I could not believe that she was afraid to tell me anything as we always had an open and honest relationship. I told her to tell me what was wrong and that I would not think she was crazy at all. She was really crying and she told me that this boy kept running into her bedroom window every night and that there was a tall man with him. My boyfriend was right there when she told me this. I grabbed her, hugged her, and told her she was not crazy. I told her that I knew all about them.

She could not believe that I had already known everything. I asked her questions to prove to my boyfriend that I was telling the truth as he did not believe in ghosts at that time and she knew everything that I had already told him. My daughter knew the whole story and she even told me that the boy told her that he used to be my best friend and that he came to me for help and I ignored him. I told her he was right. This boy began to follow her everywhere and I told her that he was not going to hurt her. She told me that he said that he would not hurt her at all.

Every day she came home from school with a different story. The same boy that had heard that girl scream heard this boy talking to my daughter one day and the boy spirit had asked my daughter a question and her friend answered the question without even realizing what had even happened. We finally helped this boy and the teacher by telling them that they must follow the light. So their spirits were finally set free.

There are so many stories like these that I could spend the rest of this book just writing about things like this. I just want to tell you that the main point of all this is to show you that everyone does have spirits around them, even if they can't see them. One day I hope that everyone can open up their minds to the idea that there is always one spirit or another that just might need your help in getting to the light above, where they belong but have lost their way. If you do believe in God for that matter, then you must believe in the spirits. God built this earth for us so he likely needs help from us, too, on occasion.

The majority of the world does believe in God so that means that we do believe in spirits, as that is what God is and he has never ever lived on this earth. In addition, there are angels as we are always told. They are also real spirits as well. They have never lived on this earth either even though some people believe that if a loved one dies that they become an angel. The deceased actually never become angels (loved ones that die have lived on this earth) and angels are always born in Heaven only and nowhere else. Over ninety percent of the world believes in these spirits so if you can learn how to open your heart to these spirits you would truly be surprised at what you can see. If you have any friends that you can truly call "best friends", as I have then you are very lucky, these are the people you can trust with anything such as advice, help, secrets, or just having fun. Over the years, a lot of people put their trust in the gods and they try to be good people. But just because you are a good person doesn't mean you will get everything you pray for. That doesn't mean that they aren't helping you, they really are, but it doesn't work like that. Everyone has to understand that everything happens for a reason. That it's not only part of their chart but by you being in his or her life also makes it a part of your chart.

If someone is sick and is going to die, it is a fact that the gods cannot save everyone. We should also understand that death is actually a gift, and you are going to the most peaceful place that you could ever even imagine. God would not cause anyone to be in a car accident for instance. That is just life. It could never be God's fault that the roads are bad or if there is a drunk driver. This means that either you should not be on the roads if you can help it or that the snow ploughs did not get the roads done early enough.

Many people think that to love someone openly and honestly is too hard to do if they have lost a lot of loved ones already. However, never give up, it is not your fault and everyone should have the opportunity of true love. So do not feel bad if things do not always turn out the way you had hoped as this happens to everyone. When I was growing up, I had so many friends over the years and I can honestly say that I have learned something new from each one of them. Even if it was not all good, it was still a learning process that made me the person that I am today.

When loved ones do die and we are angry and upset that is because either we are going to miss them or they are too young and have not had a chance to live their lives. This was decided before they came back to earth, even if it is hard to believe. Everyone does have to experience every different way of life until they have learned everything on earth that they need to know. Even if you do not believe if you ever knew that you had a past life or recall doing the same thing twice the exact same way then it is likely that you really have. If you have ever seen or felt a spirit, then the chances are that you really have.

Some people are too afraid to get too close to people for fear of losing them in the end. Those people then should stop and change their ways. For you do not get that many chances of true friendship or love. So make the most of life while you are on this earth and don't waste the time you have. People do have a habit of putting the blame in the wrong people. We create our own destiny. Maybe not with sickness but we are the ones that create pollution and wars. That is our destiny as I have learned by myself over the years.

I spent a lot of my life saying to myself "Why did this

happen to me?" Then I realized that I am strong willed and I took what was given to me and I made it work the best that I could. When I went to see a therapist she was shocked at what I had gone through since I was five. A lot of people in my situation just either gave up or ended up on the streets. Some people even ended their own life. I still thank God for helping me through this life. Love and belief that tomorrow can only get better, along with strength and good friends will make your life become that much easier. Put your life back together in order to achieve your own goals.

In my life, I can honestly say that I have five true "Best friends". Two I have known and still keep in touch with, even though we live a long way away from each other now. We have been very close to each other ever since I was only twelve. One I named my daughter after.

My Daughter Danielle Delaine

The love I give comes from my heart.
For this I ask, we shall never part.
I could only have one child, for that I am truly blessed,
As I could never imagine life without you,

As you might have already guessed.
The pain that I suffer could never compare,
To the love in our hearts that we both share.
You give love to people every day.
For that I am proud of you more then I could ever say.

You are smart and thoughtful and so very kind.
When you decide to do something, you never change your
mind.

I thank God that you have the gift of sight,
For when I die, I know you will visit me in the Heavenly
light.

I thank God for you
This precious daughter of mine.
I will love you forever and ever even after I die.
I love no one more than you, love your mommy.

8

Bringing Sight into Your Life

I have spent years doing magic but I know that black magic is not the way to go. I have spent so many years wasted by hating that now I realize that I cannot become a whole person this way. Now I still do practice magic but it is not what you might think and this way really works for the highest good of all. I have decided that you can keep living in the light all the time. It just takes practice and the knowhow.

I want to share some different ways of not just helping yourself but this can also help other people too. The first things that I have learned are: believing in God along with the angels. We all have spirit guides to help us but in the past, I did not know this. I have spent a lot of time reading but I still have not read the bible believe it or not. You can believe in yourself without reading the bible, as I did. I still have no real knowledge of the meaning of what is in the bible. I do however have some friends that go to church. So when I have visions of angels or for instance the Heavenly Mother, I just ask them. I cannot believe when I tell them things they know what I am talking about. Some are amazed and believe that the statements I make are true. It gives them that much more belief in the angels, along with other things that they are taught in church. Not to mention how much more of a believer it makes me.

Sometimes this one friend of mine will look things up in her bible and write it down to give me a better understanding of what I am seeing. Even though people go to church, that does not mean that they can actually see the things that they are taught. They might believe in what they have been taught but they are still really blinded by sight of what is always right in front of them. Like myself, I have never been taught about what is in the bible but I know that what I see and feel is true.

I would never want to put religion in the churches down, but today it seems like most churches have turned more commercialized than years ago. I do not mean to sound this way but they seem to teach you about the bible but how do we know if they really see the light in its true form? Or are they just preaching what they read? I have read many books on white magic and most of it is about how to get in touch with your spirit guides along with the angels. Out of the things that I have read, I believe that anyone can truly see the light in several different ways. I would like to explain to you some easy ways that do not seem to be difficult at all to do. In addition, magic is a very real thing that mainly just requires people to have an open mind along with an open heart that wishes well to others not only you.

When I first began to call upon the angels and my spirit guides, all I did was find a safe place in my house or outside, wherever feels best for you and think of them. Then I would take my left hand and place it on the top of my head and say, "Ariel above me" and as I did this, I would wait until I could see Ariel. Then I would place my left hand on the bottom of my stomach and say, "Michael beneath me" and I would see Michael. I would see two angels now and then Ariel would go behind me and Michael would be in front of me. After you see this put your left hand on your left shoulder and say, "Gabriel to my left" and then you would see three Angels. Then put your left hand on your right shoulder and say, "Raphael to my right". Once you have a picture of these four Angels around you then say, "By the power of you great angels, please surround me with light." After that, you will feel a great light around you. One important thing you should always do once you have reached that point is to bow your head and give thanks to each angel and repeating each of their names as you do. After that you should be able to see them, as well as be able to see a very bright light around you. That light will reach up in the sky in a cone shape with the wider end way above you. Another way you can do this is to lie down on a bed. As you lay there picture your body in another place in the room. Never try to picture yourself leaving or entering your body, just see yourself somewhere else.

After you have done that, you can ask to either see your spirit guides or ask a sick friend to be healed or you can ask pretty well any question that you choose. Never be greedy though, because the point of this is to be for the highest good of all, not just too always gain things for your self. If you want, you can meet both your spirit guides and angels, as mine always form into a circle and I always spiritually float up to them. In addition, if I want to ask for a favor for someone else I will usually wait until it is late at night. Then I will spiritually take their spirit with me after I think that they are asleep and they do not even know it. When you are done, you will float back down again. You should always bow your head and thank them again and I usually say one of two things, I will sometimes say "Blessed Be" or "So Mote It Be" either one will work.

In doing this I have also given money to a charity or you

could go through your clothes and give the ones that you don't want to the Salvation Army or you could even help others in need. Anything that won't require, thank you in return. Sometimes I even give a gift to the earth such as water or sea salt, a crystal, plant flowers or feed the birds. There are so many things that you can give of yourself that do not require any thank you in return. The main key is always to give and then you will receive. I am not saying that you cannot ask for anything for yourself as you can, but never ask for something unless you are prepared to give something in return. If you do get what you have asked for always thank the angels, along with your guide. You can receive as long as you do not take advantage of them or act selfish in return. Everything must be give and take with an open heart not a greedy mind. If you receive what you wish for always, give something of yourself in return.

If you are one of the people in this world that can just leave your body then I think you will have an easier time than others will. I have figured out how to meditate as it is mainly just visualization which everyone does at one time or another. As for your guide and Angels, when I first called them I could only see three of them. After a few months there were six, then before I knew it there were all there. Do not be surprised if this happens to you as I am sure that after a while you will see more than you would ever imagine.

I spend a lot of time either visiting my family members that have passed away and finding different ways to help others in need of one thing or another. If you tried to do things like this, you would feel so much better about yourself. I do many spells to try to help others who are sick or unhappy or if there is someone who might need extra money. Just the feeling of helping others helps me to feel whole.

After practicing calling the angles along with my guide and the Heavenly Mother, I noticed that now I do not have to call upon them whenever I need them. They are always there. For that, I am truly grateful. Helping others is not just for the living, we can also help spirits. I have spent a lot of time helping spirits that are lost and cannot seem to find their way home again. This one day, my friend and I were talking about spirits and I was telling her about how there were many spirits around that need help. At any rate, my boyfriend stopped by and we seemed to get off that particular topic. A little later on I felt a new presence in my house. It was a very strong man with a lot of anger in him. I have to say that he made me a little nervous because of the anger. After that, I began preparing my daughter's supper as she was going to be home from school shortly. I quit thinking about him for the time being. Later on, I could feel that he was getting really angry with me and I have to say that I was a bit scared of him as he was right behind me all night.

After my daughter and mother went to bed, this man really made me scared. I tried to calm him down and I told him that I wanted to help him go home. He wanted to go but in a way, he was either frightened of what might happen or he was not quite ready to leave. Right away, I called for the angels along with my guide, to help me. Just so you know, I am not talking with my voice but with my mind. Well, once I had the angels and my guide there to help me, I have to admit I was still a bit frightened. I not only wanted him to leave the house but I did want to set him free, as well. I convinced him to take my hand and that everything would be all right. I was floating upward above him and at first, I thought that he was going to come with me, but then he changed his mind and began pulling me back down again. I begged him, along with the angels and my guide to help me and they did. We all finally floated upward and we reached my guide. I was not expecting to see a swirl of wind twirl down to where he was and it just took him upward until he was above me. Then he just disappeared into the light above us. I floated back down and thanked them all for helping me. Our house was clean once again.

After that, I have been amazed at the spirits that want to go to Heaven but have lost their way somehow. I know that when I die I will definitely be heading towards the light. After that spirit was safely home, along came many other spirits, as if I had opened up something that attracted them to me for guidance. I also helped all spirits and still do on a regular basis. The only difference now is that instead of calling just my guide, I call on their guide as well.

There are many books on the market that you can read for different types of white magic that are very helpful. The spells in these books are mainly used with candles, incense, herbs, crystals, salt, and of course the calling of the angels. When I first met the Heavenly Mother,

I really did not have any idea who she was until she told me. I have never read anything about her in any of these books. The more magic you do, the more you will see and the better you get at it. Another thing was my guide, who I never read about either. If you practice white magic, you will see how much of nature is involved.

There is also air, fire, water, and salt. Sage is a very good cleansing herb that is used to bless and cleanse yourself. I always cleanse all of my ingredients along with my body to make sure that there is no negativity in anything. There are so many different spells to heal or protect anyone along with your self. I believe that the main thing that you should always do is to give something back in return for anything that you wish for. Even if you do a spell to help someone else, always offer even water or flower seeds to the earth. You can perform any spell that has to do with giving with an open heart or if it is for the highest good for all. Never be greedy as it will come back on you if you do not give as you have received.

I have also used many different kinds of tarot cards which can offer some guidance but I prefer to put my trust in the gods instead. Tarot cards sometimes give off too much negativity. If anyone feels empty or even dark inside, trust me as that used to be me. I know how it feels to feel nothing inside but either hate or just plain numb. Just remember, this is your life so do not let people get you down. You always have to find the strength in yourself as that is really the only person that you can trust and count on. At one time in my life I truly drank a lot but then one night I watched all the drunks around me and that made me stop and think twice about what I was doing to myself.

That was over twenty-five years ago and I still had many things to learn about myself. Everyone who has gone through a bad experience in their life should stop and think of the things that could have happened to you and think to yourself that a lot worse things might have happened including death. I am grateful that I did not hate the world for what I thought was a very bad life. As it turned out, I realized how lucky I was that I lived through everything and have grown into the person I am today. I hope and pray that you can see the good in yourself as I did.

I cannot believe that the terrorists attacked on September 11, 2001 as they killed thousands of innocent people. We now have been at war with them ever since that day. They want freedom so they kill to get it, but it would never be that way. Everyone wants freedom and we are blessed for the freedom that we have in Canada along with the United States. You would think that there was enough earth to go around for everyone to be happy but apparently, that is never the case. If you think about it we are also killing the earth and this is what the whole war started over-freedom. How many innocent people have to die until we are truly free? Why do these terrorists kill everyone? Even the people that our governments allow to live in these countries make plans on how to kill us. This I do not understand. Some of these terrorists have lived in our countries for over ten years. Then all of a sudden they turn on us and kill innocent people. This cannot bring them freedom as they just cause war and hate which makes it hard for their people who live in our countries to live in peace. Peace for them is getting everything that they want with no care or concern for anyone else in the world. I believe that we should never have to live in fear as many people do now.

God did not create this world for people to hate and kill. What- ever happened to peace and harmony? We are not here to kill God's children as that is a true crime. This land was made for everyone to share and there is more than enough to go around. We should stop and think what we are doing before the earth as we know it, becomes extinct. We have accomplished so much in all of these years. So why destroy everything we have learned? Why can't we end this war? Aren't we all just one big family? Let blinded eyes finally see that to love our neighbors will set us all free.

9

The Healing Process

I guess you could say that I have tried just about anything to heal myself. I always tried to be friendly to everyone and I think that helped my state of mind. I figured that I have been healing myself for many years now. I have to admit that it is a very slow process. Once I was rid of the shame and realized that this was not at all my fault and that he was sick. It seemed a little easier for me. I was just a child so there was no way that I had anything to do with what was going on in his head. I had a strict father in one hand and a very nice one in the other. We all had to do everything that he said or else there was hell to pay. I had no choice but to do what I was told and I knew it.

As I became a teenager I felt like killing myself so many times but at the same time I still wanted to live. I wanted to leave and never come back, but I had no money and I had nowhere to go so I could not bring myself to do that either. I now understand why so many children end up on the streets. The problem with that is that if you have no money then you end up afraid and selling your body for sex anyway. If you were afraid before then think how much more it would be on the streets. I cannot say that I blame them for wanting a way out but I just could not bring myself to do that so I stayed instead. I always figured that I would rather suffer at home and still be with my family than to have no one at all so I stayed. I did start to spend a lot of time at my friends though where I knew it was safe which did help a lot.

I was in school and missing a lot of time. I might add, I even went to the counselor for help but they did nothing for me. I talked to one of my favorite teachers too, but he did nothing. I was even on nerve pills when I was fourteen and all of the doctors knew and they did nothing either. I used to wonder why no one seemed to care what I was going through but I now think that it was just that time. Today the people do not get away with it as much as they used to. I have to admit that back then, I was too afraid to go into details about what really happened. In a way I still am because to this day no one knows everything but me.

When I was young, I wrote a book about every time and every date that my father would molest me. One day he found it in my room and took it away from me. Boy was he ever mad at me for that! He never said anything to me about the book. He just stood there and glared at me as if he was going to kill me and I actually thought he just might do that. That book seemed to help me release some of my anger. So after that, I started writing letters to him instead. But after I wrote them I ripped them up so he would never see them again. This did help to get my anger out but if it were now I think I would have given them to him as long as I was not living at home with him. I think that as long as you are out of the house and are protected that they should know exactly what they did and how it made you feel.

Another idea is if you have a tape recorder and tape everything that they say to you so you have proof to take to the police. I think that might have helped me earlier in life. If you get the chance to buy one, do it. Then call the police. I find they take it more seriously now then back then. If you call the police and they don't do anything then keep calling every chance you get. Then tell them you want an internal examination to be done, if they do not believe you. If you do that, make sure you do not shower no matter how much you want to. Just do not do it! Tell the police you want to charge whoever it may be. If by chance, they still don't do anything then the only option would be to go to the hospital, and tell them you were raped. Then the hospital has to call the police and usually charges are placed because the hospital has to check you over.

If things get so bad that you cannot stand it, find some kind of support group, or an abuse center. I had to go to therapy for over a year and a half. When I went there, I did not think anything would become of it; however, they gave me different assignments to do every week. It did not cost me anything and it was called Alternatives. I did the assignments but I did not tell her everything about what had happened to me, because I still felt dirty inside.

I started opening up more and talking more about things that happened as I grew older. The pain seems to lessen over the years that have gone by, which makes it easier to talk about. I think it is because you can get away from the person the older you get. In addition, you do not have to face that person everyday if you do not want to. Some people do not ever half to face the people again. I only wish that was so my case. However, what you do remember many people do go through this so always keep in mind that you are not the only one. The more you can open up and talk about the abuse, the better you will feel. If you feel like there is no one you can go to. Stop! There are always abuse centers, and they can even find you a place to stay. You never have to be alone. Never be too proud to ask for help, because that is what they are there for.

If you are lucky enough, you get justice and the person is sent to jail, you will begin to feel better inside. Anything that you can do to make yourself feel better do it, but remember two wrongs do not make it right. Revenge is never the way to go. You do not want to be the one who ends up in jail, because of what they did to you. Let the judge decide their punishment. Why would you want to end up in jail? That will make them feel like they have to turn the tables on you. Always think smart because if they went to jail, the inmates would turn on them because they do not like child abuse. Every boyfriend I ever had I remember I was ashamed of my body because of what happened. I thought for years that I even hated men. I thought that they were cold-hearted people and all they ever wanted was sex.

I did not think men even ever knew the meaning of love. It took me years to even talk to them and even try to understand them. I never wanted them to see my naked body. I was still ashamed of what happened. I thought sex was dirty and just another chore of womanhood. Once I realized I could just say no, I felt a lot better. Men do not own us! We own ourselves! We decide when the time is right, not them. That was one of the best feelings I had, the thought that I actually owned my life and no one else would ever own me again. That gave me the feeling of self worth. That was a very valuable lesson for me.

If you are in a relationship where your man controls you and makes you feel like your nothing but a tool to them, then get out! Turn the tables and tell them to go to hell. You control your body and your life. No one can take that from you. You should never be told what to do or listen to those who tell you to do things that you do not want to do. Take control! Listen to your inner self. If you're inner self tells you to leave then leave. Never forget that because when you take power over your own life, then you will finally become free. I never thought I would ever be free even though it took me many years to find freedom. It was well worth it. Now I can actually get up in the morning and not be frightened. I can do whatever I want. I will never trade my freedom for anyone other than my daughter ever again.

So if you have to take orders and do as someone else tells you, take a long look at yourself and figure out what you want out of life then do it. I broke free and my daughter was the reason. Now I live a happy life. Even with responsibilities, I still live in peace. No longer am I afraid to come home for fear of what some man wants from me. If I want to love a man and I do, then that is purely my choice. I now know the true meaning of life-that is love and happiness. My soul is finally free and for that, I am thankful.

I often thought that I was fortunate in one way that I didn't get pregnant by my father. I really don't know what I would have done. If you think about it, some people are not so lucky. On one hand you have a life inside you, but could you really have a baby that was conceived by rape. I really cannot say what I would have done. I mean it is not the baby's fault. Then again, could you have the baby and keep it? I think that would be hard, you would likely wonder if the baby would have his traits of abuse or not. Would you resent the baby because of what happened to you? That would have to be one of the hardest decisions anyone would have to make. I think you would have to have a lot of courage inside of you. If you gave the baby up for adoption, at least the child would have a chance of having a good life with someone else. Even still, if you could have an abortion then that might bother you too. It would take a strong person to live with either of these choices. There is no right or wrong answer in either situation because it would depend on how it would make you feel.

Any answer is right if you, yourself can live in peace with your decision. Never feel guilty or shameful, as you are the one who will live with it, no one else. In order to be free, I would have to say that you have to be open-hearted with your decision. Be true to only yourself. Never feel like you have to do what anyone else tells you to do. Just do what your heart tells you to, and do not worry about it, it is different for everyone. Try not to spend the rest of your life with the choice you made-trust your decision, it is the right one. The one most important thing that will set you free is forgiveness. This might be hard to understand but eventually you will reach peace by practicing forgiveness. This may be a long process, but it is necessary and with patience and diligence, your pain can be transformed by letting go of past wounds. It is the only way to a peaceful heart and soul.

I made my own checklist of things which some people go through before they are healed:

- Get rid of any shame in your heart-remember this was not your fault, as they have a medical illness.
- Instead of depression, seek help in any way that you can. Try to stay happy even if you are sad, even if you're only pretending. This will enable you to cope. Dwelling on the negative will only increase your depression.
- Healing can be a very slow process, be patient.
- Keep fighting and never give up.
- Talk to a trusted family member or friend—if no one is listening keep talking.
- Write down as many feelings as you can—even write a letter to the abuser whether you give it to them or not.
- If you have a tape recorder, record it for evidence. Phone the police for help if they do nothing do not give up, keep calling.

- Go to the hospital without showering and tell them you were sexually assaulted. The hospital is obligated to call the police with any evidence the medical staff uncovers.
- Search for a support group for help. Go to the nearest abuse centre and if you have no financial support go to social services.
- Never take revenge out on the abuser, this will only increase the pain you suffer and any attempt may result in you going to prison. Let the police and the court system decide the punishment for the abuser. Two wrongs do not make a right.
- Never let anyone control you. Take control over your own life. Decide your options without anyone's interference and make your decisions with careful thought.
- If you are pregnant, you need to decide what is best for you. Keep in mind that you will have to live with your own decision. Do not be influenced by others.
- Talk about it as much as you can-this is a key to understanding which will lead to forgiveness, which will lead you to peace.
- The Light shall set you free.

I also want to give you some ideas that might help you whether you are a child or an adult in an abusive relationship. If you have a video camera set it up in a place where the abuser usually strikes: to catch them in the act. Keep putting it there until you are attacked then when you get a chance to take the tape out and hide it somewhere outside of the house where it cannot be found. Even if that means putting it in a lot of plastic zip lock bags and finding a safe place to bury it until you are safe enough to dig it up and take it to the police.

Another thing you could do is if you are in an abusive

relationship is to try to save some of the grocery money and hide it outside of the house. I would not put it in the bank in a separate account, he might find it somehow. If you give it to a friend they might need to borrow it for some reason and they might not have it when you need it. Always try to keep what you are doing a secret. Someone you know might accidentally let something slip when the abuser is around and that would be the end of it, and of course it would be trouble for you and no one else. If you are a child save your allowance, birthday and Christmas money if you can. I do hope that you can talk to your mother about the abuse and that your mother would believe you. Then she could help you. Children do not usually make up things like that so please believe your child and do everything in your power to help and protect them.

If you can, you should try to find a way to take a self-defense class.

If you are a stay-at-home mother, try to do it during the day and if that is not possible, find away to go out at night somehow. Say that you are going to your parent's house and if he insists on coming along with you then talk to your mother and see if she will help you get out of the house. Better still, she could go with you for added protection if that is possible. If these things do not work and you cannot find anywhere to go then you will have to go to a shelter, that is what they are there for. They will keep you safe and they will not tell anyone that you are there. If this is your only choice then make sure ahead of time that you have the main things that you need already packed. If you have to call the police, then let them escort you out so that he cannot do anything to you while you leave. Always think one step ahead of him because if he will not let you go then you will have to be sneakier then him.

Remember the more times that you call the police or go to the hospital, then the more times it will be on record. That will give you a step up from him, as they will already know what he is capable of. If he is a stalker and you have a restraining order on him and he follows you and tries to get you then think a step ahead of him and set traps to keep him out of your house. Set as many as you can and get an alarm system to scare him away.

At least that might give you enough time until the police get there. In addition, scream for help at the top of your lungs. That should scare him away as he might think that someone will come and help you. The whole idea to this is that if you can think of any way to get him back instead of being afraid all of your life, then do it. You have to fight fire with fire in order to win! The more frightened that you are, the easier chance he has to get you. One more thing to always do is to have a weapon that you can use on him. The more you beat him down the easier for you to survive. Most importantly, do not be afraid. It is just self-defense. If he is on your property trying to attack you, fight back. Just do not kill him or you will end up in jail. Just try to survive as you have the right to live just like everyone else and please never forget that. Revenge is not the answer so do not go after him unless he is the one trying to harm you.

I hope that you never have to spend your life in fear.

May God be with you. Blessed Be.

Heaven's Light

Up in heavens
What a beautiful sight
Once you are healed
You will finally see the Light

Call upon the Angels
To set your soul free
There are no words
For the love that you feel

Keep love in your heart and things will get better
If things go bad, as they sometimes do
Call upon the Angels
As they are always there to guide you

Blessed be.

The End

Summary

Let us heal ourselves from hurt and pain.
Give us strength and courage to live again.
If we allow abuse to overpower us,
Then you will never know whom you can trust.
Have faith in yourself so you can grow
Into the person, you thought you would never know.
Give strength and wisdom in all that you do.
Then the light will shine down upon you.
If love is what your heart desires,
Then trust in yourself and you will be inspired.
The key to life is freedom, you see,
Believe in yourself so Blessed Be.

About The Author

Hi! My name is Cheryl Jolly.

I feel that I am qualified to write this book as I am just a person who has lived in fear for many years. My father was an alcoholic and a mean, threatening man. I was sexually abused from the time I was five until over fifteen years of age. I have been to many doctors and so was my father. I not only lived in fear but I was frightened for my life.

This book is to help anyone and also to raise money for abuse centers worldwide. I suffer from many diseases and I am disabled due to the severe pain that I live with daily. I am a survivor and I want to help anyone else that I can have the strength to fight and survive to live a better and happier life as I have done.